A Decade of Lite
Contemporary Pop Ballads

Arranged by
DAN COATES

Project Manager: Carol Cuellar
Editorial Assistant: Donna Salzburg
Book Art Layout: Design O'Rama

DAN COATES® is a registered trademark of Warner Bros. Publications

Contents

Dan Coates ❑❑❑❑❑❑❑❑❑❑❑❑❑❑❑❑❑❑

As a student at the University of Miami, Dan Coates paid his tuition by playing the piano at south Florida nightclubs and restaurants. One evening in 1975, after Dan had worked his unique brand of magic on the ivories, a stranger from the music field walked up and told him that he should put his inspired piano arrangements down on paper so they could be published.

Dan took the stranger's advice—and the world of music has become much richer as a result. Since that chance encounter long ago, Dan has gone on to achieve international acclaim for his brilliant piano arrangements. His *Big Note, Easy Piano* and *Professional Touch* arrangements have inspired countless piano students and established themselves as classics against which all other works must be measured.

Enjoying an exclusive association with Warner Bros. Publications since 1982, Dan has demonstrated a unique gift for writing arrangements intended for students of every level, from beginner to advanced. Dan never fails to bring a fresh and original approach to his work. Pushing his own creative boundaries with each new manuscript, he writes material that is musically exciting and educationally sound.

From the very beginning of his musical life, Dan has always been eager to seek new challenges. As a five-year-old in Syracuse, New York, he used to sneak into the home of his neighbors to play their piano. Blessed with an amazing ear for music, Dan was able to imitate the melodies of songs he had heard on the radio. Finally, his neighbors convinced his parents to buy Dan his own piano. At that point, there was no stopping his musical development. Dan won a prestigious New York State competition for music composers at the age of 15. Then, after graduating from high school, he toured the world as an arranger and pianist with the group Up With People.

Later, Dan studied piano at the University of Miami with the legendary Ivan Davis, developing his natural abilities to stylize music on the keyboard. Continuing to perform professionally during and after his college years, Dan has played the piano on national television and at the 1984 Summer Olympics in Los Angeles. He has also accompanied recording artists as diverse as Dusty Springfield and Charlotte Rae.

During his long and prolific association with Warner Bros. Publications, Dan has written many award-winning books. He conducts piano workshops worldwide, demonstrating his famous arrangements with a special spark that never fails to inspire students and teachers alike.

ALL MY LIFE

Words and Music by
RORY BENNETT and
JO JO HAILEY
Arranged by DAN COATES

1. I will nev-er find an-oth-er lov-er sweet-er than you, sweet-er than you. And

I will nev-er find an-oth-er lov-er more pre-cious than you, more pre-cious than you. Girl, you are

6

close to me, you're like my moth - er, close to me, you're like my fath - er. Close to me, you're like my sis - ter,

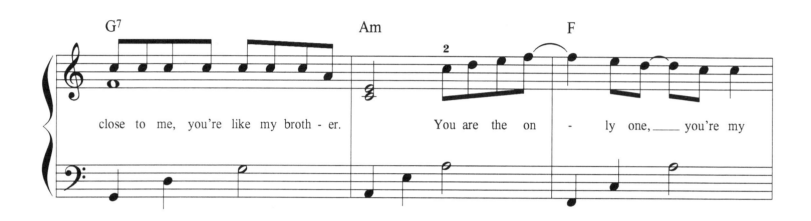

close to me, you're like my broth - er.   You are the on - ly one, ___ you're my

Chorus:

ev - 'ry - thing, and for you this song ___ I sing. All   my   life, ___   I

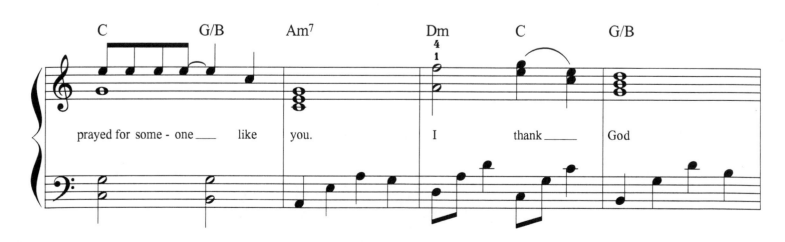

prayed for some - one ___ like you.   I   thank ___   God

7

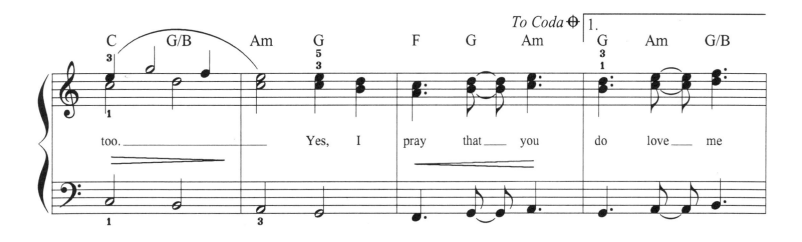

All My Life - 5 - 3

8

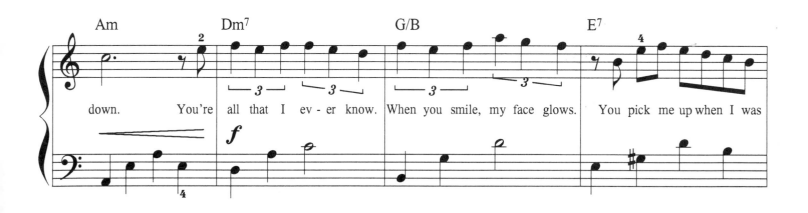

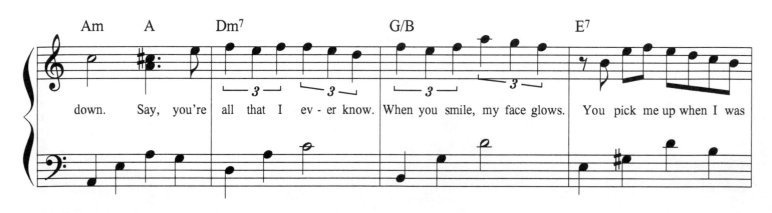

Verse 2:
I promise to never fall in love with a stranger.
You're all I'm thinking of,
I praise the Lord above
For sending me your love.
I cherish every hug.
I really love you.
(To Chorus:)

ALL BY MYSELF

Words and Music by
ERIC CARMEN and **SERGEI RACHMANINOFF**
Arranged by DAN COATES

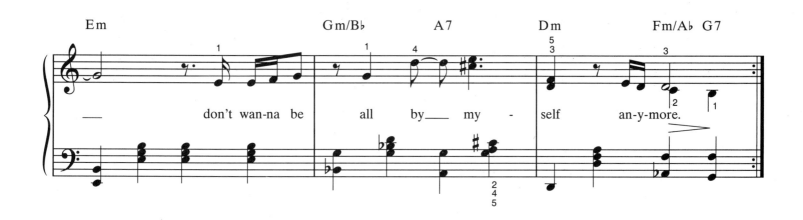

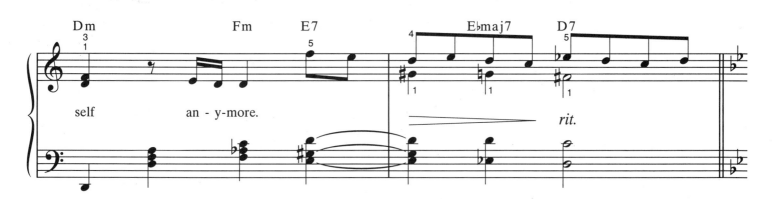

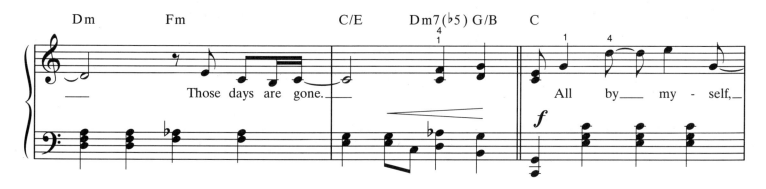

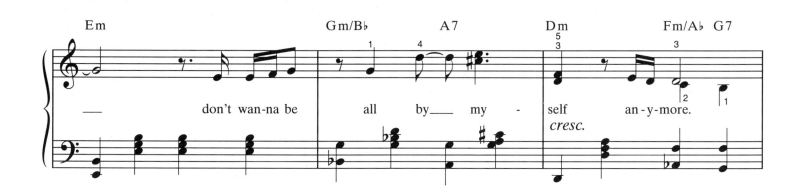

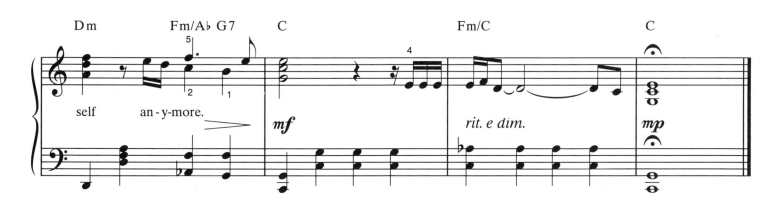

ALL I HAVE TO GIVE

Words and Music by
FULL FORCE
Arranged by DAN COATES

Moderately slow, with a steady beat

Verse:

1. I don't know what he does to make you cry, but I'll be there to make you smile. I don't have a fan - cy car to get to you, I'd walk a thou - sand miles. I don't care

I have ___ to give. ___ With - out you I don't ___ think I ___ can live. ___

I wish I could give ___ the world ___ to you, ___ but love is all I

have to give. ___   But my love is all ___   *rit. e dim.*

Verse 2:
When you talk, does it seem like he's not
Even listening to a word you say?
That's okay, baby, just tell me your problems.
I'll try my best to kiss them all away.
Does he leave when you need him the most
'Cause his friends get all your time?
Baby, please, I'm on my knees
Praying for the day that you'll be mine.
(To Chorus:)

ALWAYS AND FOREVER

Words and Music by
ROD TEMPERTON
Arranged by DAN COATES

1. Al - ways and for - ev - er, ____ each mo -ment with you
2. There'll al - ways be sun - shine ____ when I look at you.

is just like a dream to me that some - how came true.
Some - thing I can't ex - plain, just the things that you do.

And I know to - mor - row ____ will still be the same,
And if you get lone - ly, ____ call me and take

Always and Forever - 3 - 1

Always and Forever - 3 - 3

AMAZED

Words and Music by
MARV GREEN, AIMEE MAYO
and CHRIS LINDSEY
Arranged by DAN COATES

I can hear your thoughts, I can see your ___ dreams.

Chorus:

I don't know how you do what you do. ___ I'm so in love with

you. It just keeps get-ting bet - ter.

I wan-na spend the rest of my life ___ with you by my side ___

Amazed - 5 - 3

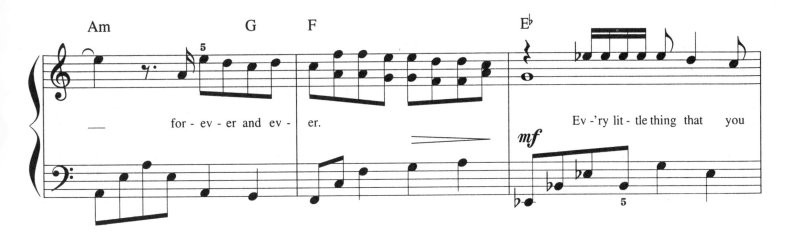

Verse 2:
The smell of your skin,
The taste of your kiss,
The way you whisper in the dark.
Your hair all around me,
Baby, you surround me.
You touch every place in my heart.
Oh, it feels like the first time every time.
I wanna spend the whole night in your eyes.
(To Chorus:)

Amazed - 5 - 5

ANGEL EYES

Composed by
JIM BRICKMAN
Arranged by DAN COATES

Angel Eyes - 3 - 1

Angel Eyes - 3 - 2

28

ANGEL OF MINE

Words and Music by
RHETT LAWRENCE and TRAVON POTTS
Arranged by DAN COATES

Angel of Mine - 5 - 1

32

Angel of Mine - 5 - 4

AS LONG AS YOU LOVE ME

Words and Music by
MAX MARTIN
Arranged by DAN COATES

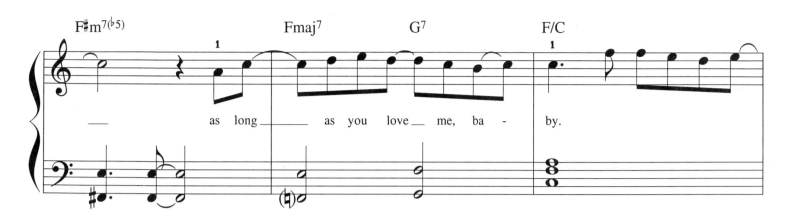

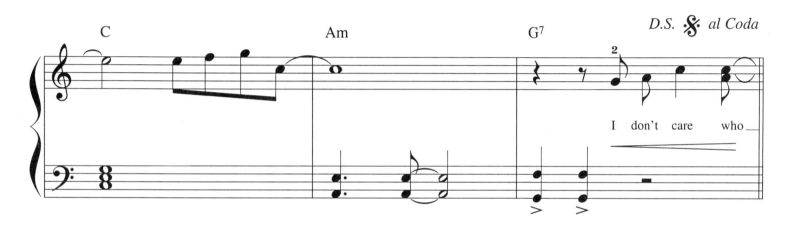

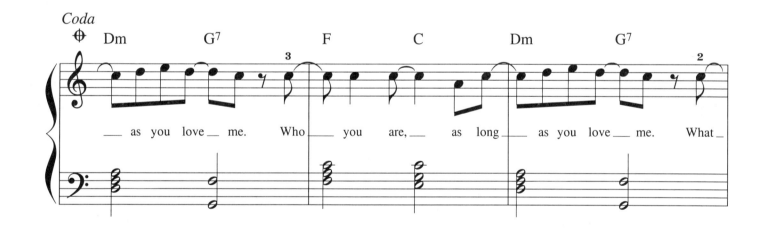

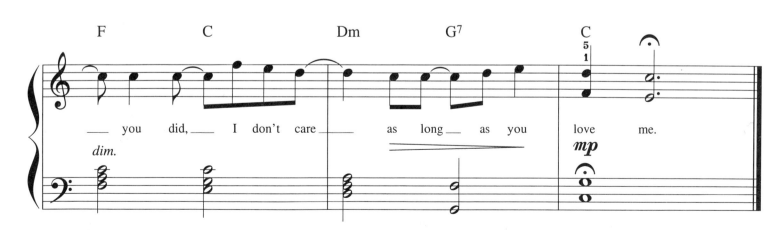

As Long As You Love Me - 4 - 4

BACK AT ONE

Words and Music by
BRIAN McKNIGHT
Arranged by DAN COATES

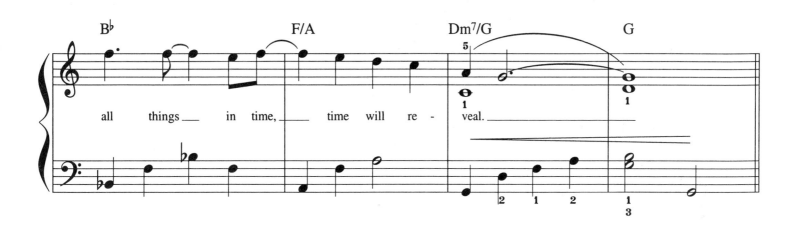

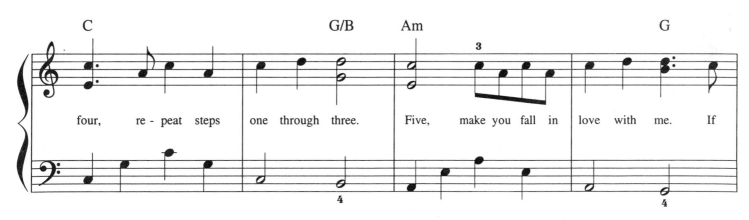

Back at One - 4 - 2

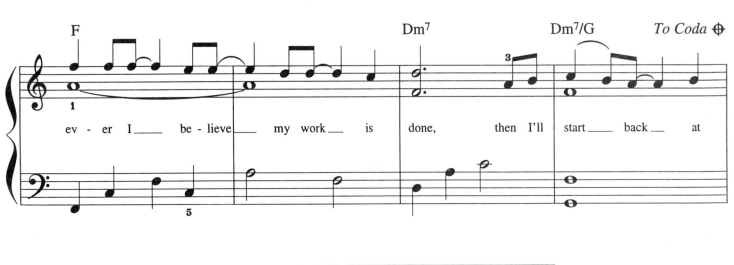

lone - ly heart___ of mine.___ You threw out___ the life - line, just

cresc.

in the nick___ of time.___

D.S. 𝄋 *al Coda*

Coda

one.___

dim.

mp   *rit.*   *p*

Verse 2:
It's so incredible,
The way things work themselves out.
And all emotional
Once you know what it's all about.
And undesirable
For us to be apart.
I never would have made it very far,
'Cause you know you've got the keys to my heart.
(To Chorus:)

BECAUSE OF YOU

Words and Music by
ANDERS BAGGE, ARNTHOR BIRGISSON,
CHRISTIAN KARLSSON and PATRICK TUCKER
Arranged by DAN COATES

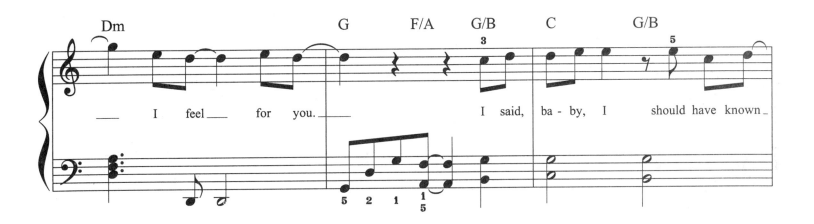

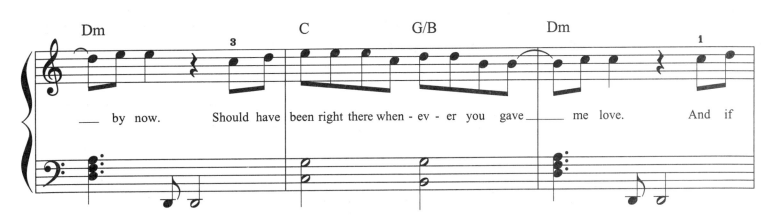

44

Because of You - 4 - 3

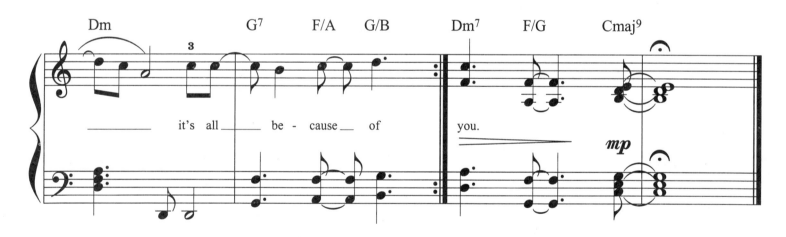

Verse 2:
Honestly, could it be you and me
Like it was before, need less or more?
'Cause when I close my eyes at night,
I realize that no one else
Could ever take your place.
I still can feel, and it's so real,
When you're touching me,
Kisses endlessly.
It's just a place in the sun
Where our love's begun.
I miss you,
Yes, I miss you.
(To Chorus:)

Because of You - 4 - 4

Theme from "UP CLOSE & PERSONAL"

BECAUSE YOU LOVED ME

Words and Music by
DIANE WARREN
Arranged by DAN COATES

48

Because You Loved Me - 5 - 3

Because You Loved Me - 5 - 4

50

BUTTERFLY KISSES

Words and Music by
BOB CARLISLE and RANDY THOMAS
Arranged by DAN COATES

Slowly and tenderly

1. There's

one thing I know for sure, she was sent here from heav - en and she's

dad - dy's lit - tle girl. As I drop to my knees by her bed at night,

Butterfly Kisses - 5 - 1

52

she talks to Je - sus, ____ and I close my eyes. And I thank God for all of the

joy in my life. Oh, but most of all, for

Chorus:

but - ter - fly kiss - es af - ter bed - time prayer, ____ stick - in'

lit - tle white flow - ers all up in her ____ hair.

54

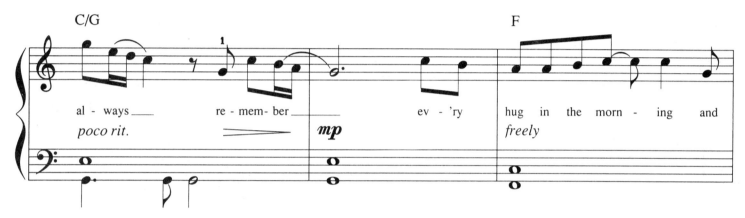

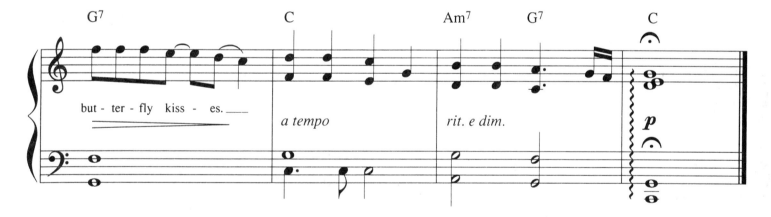

Verse 2:
Sweet sixteen today,
She's lookin' like her mama a little more every day.
One part woman, the other part girl;
To perfume and make-up from ribbons and curls.
Trying her wings out in a great big world.
But I remember:

Chorus 2:
Butterfly kisses after bedtime prayer,
Stickin' little white flowers all up in her hair.
"You know how much I love you, daddy, but if you don't mind,
I'm only gonna kiss you on the cheek this time."
Oh, with all that I've done wrong, I must have done something right
To deserve her love every morning
And butterfly kisses at night.

Verse 3:
She'll change her name today.
She'll make a promise, and I'll give her away.
Standing in the brideroom just staring at her,
She asks me what I'm thinking, and I say, "I'm not sure.
I just feel like I'm losing my baby girl."
Then she leaned over and gave me...

Chorus 3:
Butterfly kisses with her mama there,
Stickin' little white flowers all up in her hair.
"Walk me down the aisle, daddy, it's just about time."
"Does my wedding gown look pretty, daddy? Daddy, don't cry."
Oh, with all that I've done wrong, I must have done something right
To deserve her love every morning
And butterfly kisses.   *(Coda)*

BREATHE

Words and Music by
STEPHANIE BENTLEY
and **HOLLY LAMAR**
Arranged by DAN COATES

Slowly (♩ = 60)

Verse 1:

1. I can feel the mag - ic float - ing in the air;____

be - ing with you gets me that way.

I watch the sun-light dance a- | cross your face____ and I've

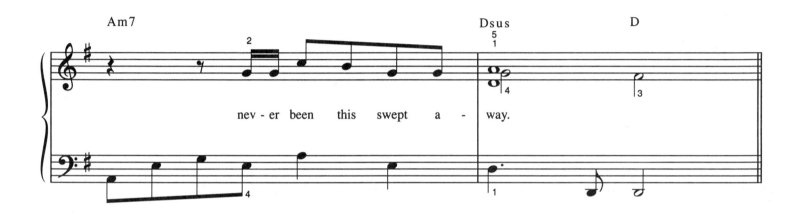

nev-er been this swept a- | way.

Verses 2 & 3:

2. All my thoughts just seem to set-tle | on the breeze____
3. In a way, I know my heart is | wak - ing up_____

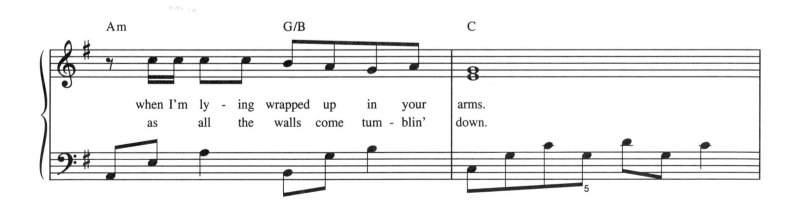

when I'm ly-ing wrapped up in your | arms.
as all the walls come tum-blin' | down.

Breathe - 6 - 2

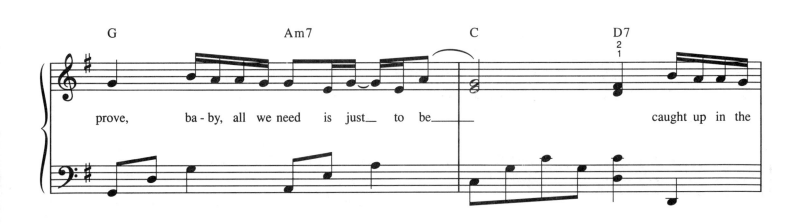

Breathe - 6 - 4

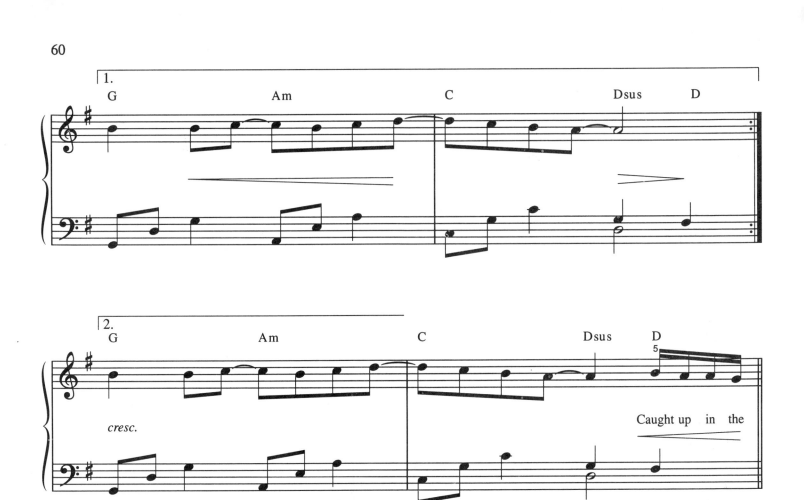

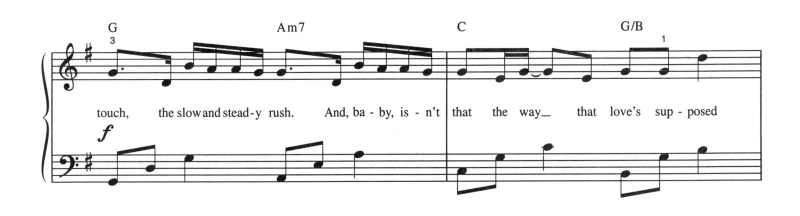

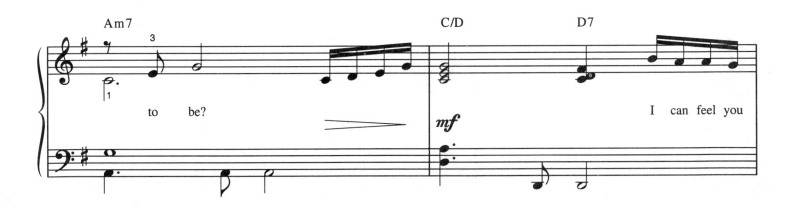

BY HEART

Composed by
JIM BRICKMAN and
HOLLYE LEVEN
Arranged by DAN COATES

CANDLE IN THE WIND

Words and Music by
ELTON JOHN and BERNIE TAUPIN
Arranged by DAN COATES

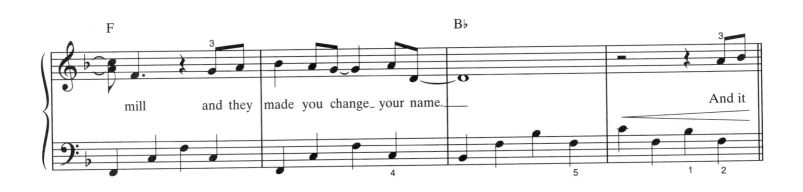

set in.___ And I would have liked___ to have known___

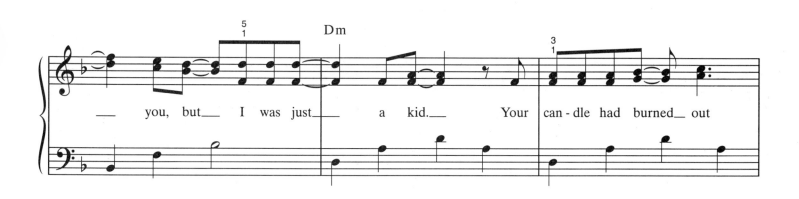

you, but___ I was just___ a kid.___ Your can-dle had burned___ out

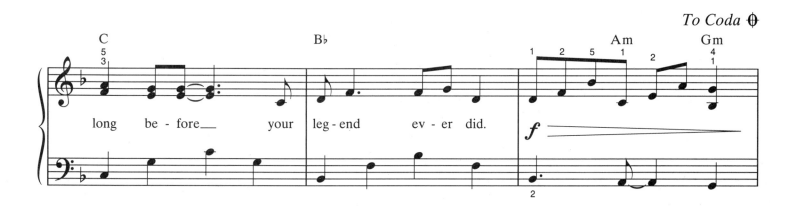

To Coda ⊕

long be-fore___ your leg-end ev-er did.

3. Good-bye, Nor - ma Jean.___ Though I nev - er knew you at all,___

4. *See additional lyrics*

mp

___ you had___ the grace to hold your-self___ while those a - round___ you crawled.___

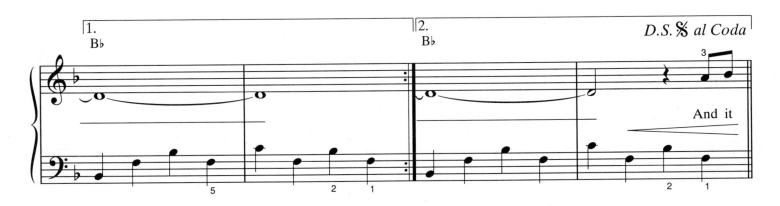

1.
B♭

2.
B♭

D.S. 𝄌 al Coda

And it

Verse 2:
Loneliness was tough,
The toughest role you ever played.
Hollywood created a superstar
And pain was the price you paid.
Even when you died,
Oh, the press still hounded you.
All the papers had to say
Was that Marilyn was found in the nude.
(To Chorus:)

Verse 4:
Goodbye, Norma Jean,
From the young man in the twenty-second row
Who sees you as something more than sexual,
More than just Marilyn Monroe.
(To Chorus:)

CHANGE THE WORLD

Words and Music by
TOMMY SIMS, GORDON KENNEDY
and WAYNE KIRKPATRICK
Arranged by DAN COATES

Change the World - 4 - 1

72

73

Change the World - 4 - 4

COUNT ON ME

Words and Music by
BABYFACE, WHITNEY HOUSTON
and MICHAEL HOUSTON
Arranged by DAN COATES

Count on me through thick and thin, a friend-ship that will nev-er end. When you are weak, I will be strong, help-ing you to car-ry on. Call on me, I will be there. Don't be a-fraid. Please be-lieve me when I say count on.

Count on Me - 5 - 1

78

Count on Me - 5 - 5

From the Twentieth Century-Fox Motion Picture "ONE FINE DAY"

FOR THE FIRST TIME

Words and Music by
JAMES NEWTON HOWARD,
ALLAN RICH and JUD FRIEDMAN
Arranged by DAN COATES

For the First Time - 5 - 1

80

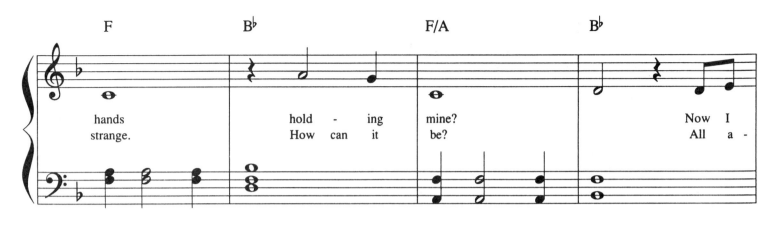

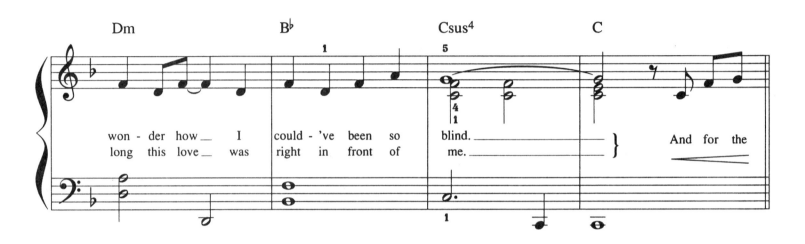

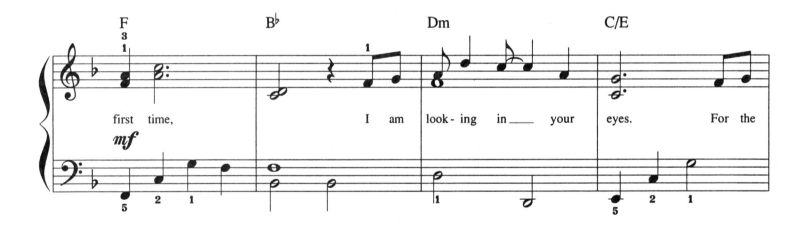

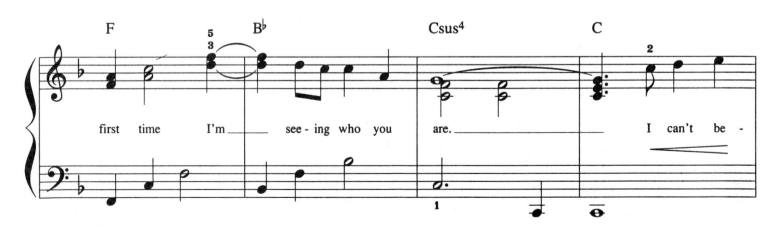

For the First Time - 5 - 2

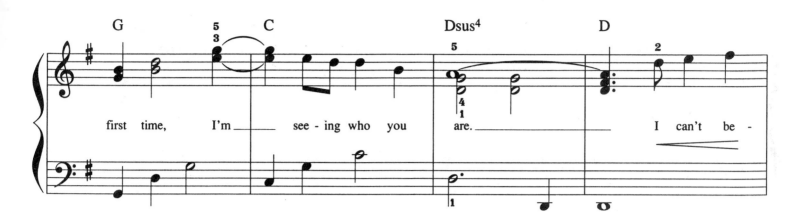

first time, I'm_____ see - ing who you are._____ I can't be -

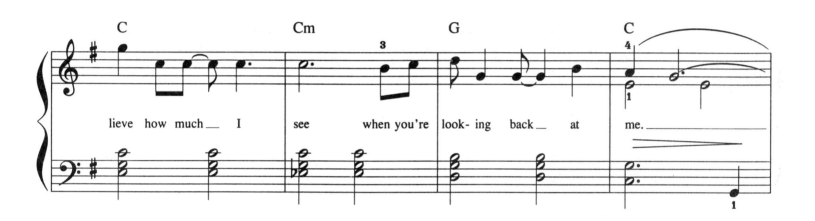

lieve how much____ I see when you're look- ing back____ at me._____

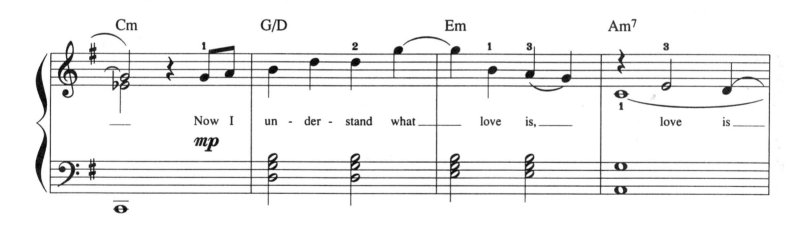

Now I un - der - stand what____ love is,_____ love is____

mp

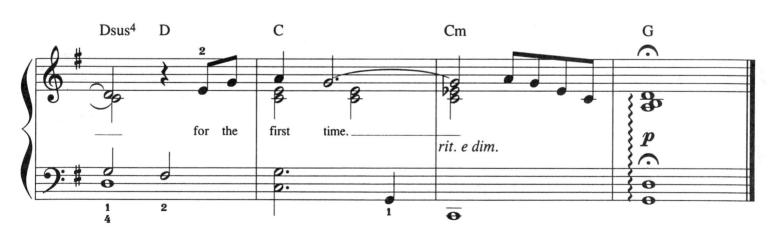

for the first time._____ *rit. e dim.* *p*

For the First Time - 5 - 5

DON'T CRY FOR ME ARGENTINA

From the Opera "EVITA"

Music by ANDREW LLOYD WEBBER
Lyrics by TIM RICE
Arranged by DAN COATES

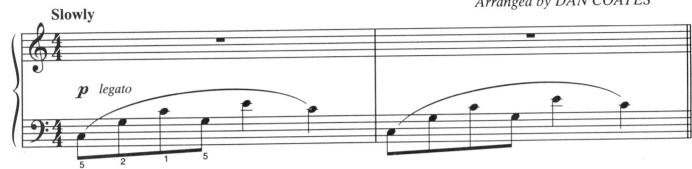

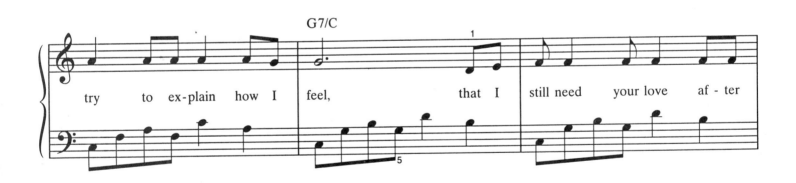

Don't Cry for Me Argentina - 4 - 1

86

Don't Cry for Me Argentina - 4 - 3

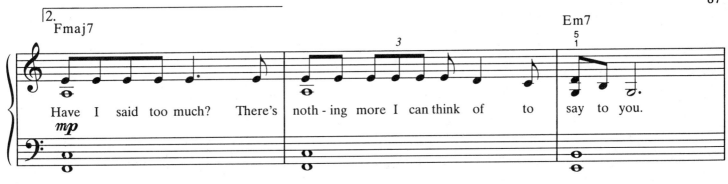

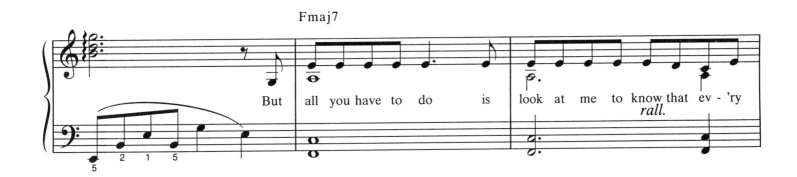

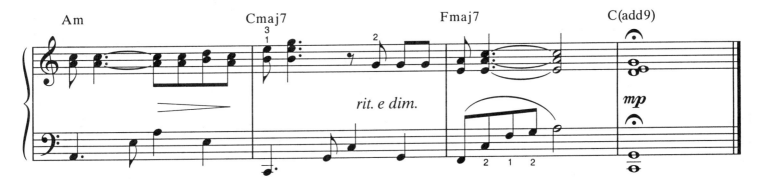

Don't Cry for Me Argentina - 4 - 4

DREAMING OF YOU

Words and Music by
TOM SNOW and
FRAN GOLDE
Arranged by DAN COATES

Dreaming of You - 4 - 1

FOOLISH GAMES

Words and Music by
JEWEL KILCHER
Arranged by DAN COATES

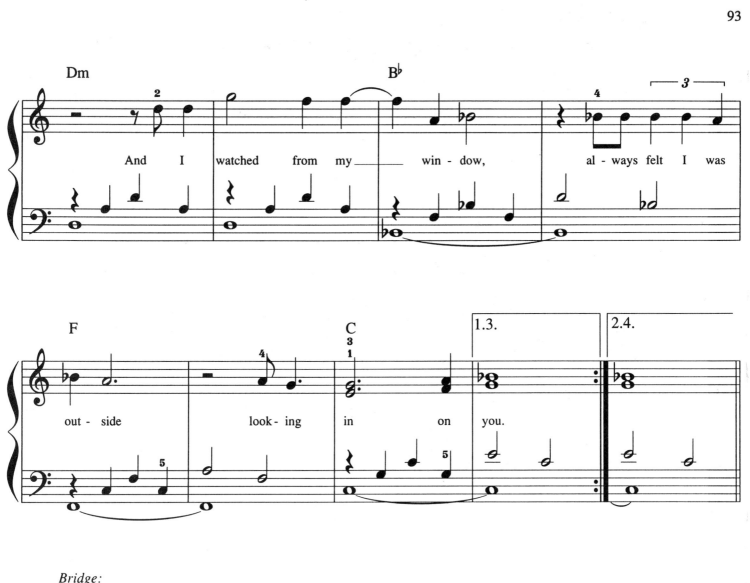

94

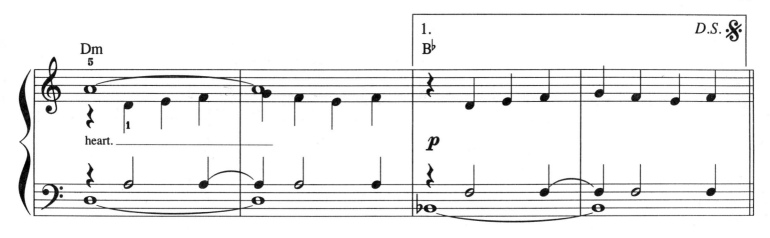

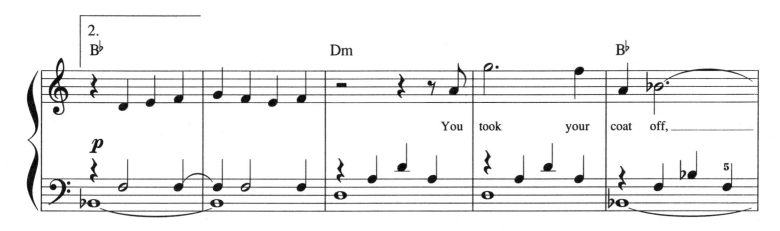

Verse 2:
You're always the mysterious one
With dark eyes and careless hair,
You were fashionably sensitive
But too cool to care.
You stood in my doorway with nothing to say
Besides some comment on the weather.
(To Bridge:)

Verse 3:
You're always brilliant in the morning,
Smoking your cigarettes and talking over coffee.
Your philosophies on art, Baroque moved you.
You loved Mozart and you'd speak of your loved ones
As I clumsily strummed my guitar.

Verse 4:
You'd teach me of honest things,
Things that were daring, things that were clean.
Things that knew what an honest dollar did mean.
I hid my soiled hands behind my back.
Somewhere along the line,
I must have gone off track with you.

Bridge 2:
Excuse me, I think I've mistaken you
For somebody else,
Somebody who gave a damn,
Somebody more like myself.
(To Chorus:)

FOR YOU I WILL

Words and Music by
DIANE WARREN
Arranged by DAN COATES

For You I Will - 4 - 1

97

For You I Will - 4 - 2

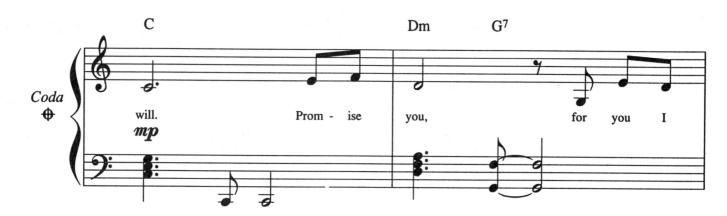

Verse 2:
I will shield your heart from the rain,
I won't let no harm come your way.
Oh, these arms will be your shelter,
No, these arms won't let you down.
If there is a mountain to move,
I will move that mountain for you.
I'm here for you, I'm here forever.
I will be a fortress, tall and strong.
I'll keep you safe, I'll stand beside you,
Right or wrong.   *(To Chorus:)*

FROM THIS MOMENT ON

Words and Music by
SHANIA TWAIN and R.J. LANGE
Arranged by DAN COATES

From This Moment On - 3 - 1

102

Verse 3:
From this moment, as long as I live,
I will love you, I promise you this.
There is nothing I wouldn't give,
From this moment on.

Chorus 2:
You're the reason I believe in love.
And you're the answer to my prayers from up above.
All we need is just the two of us.
My dreams came true
Because of you.

From This Moment On - 3 - 3

HANDS

Words and Music by
JEWEL KILCHER and
PATRICK LEONARD
Arranged by DAN COATES

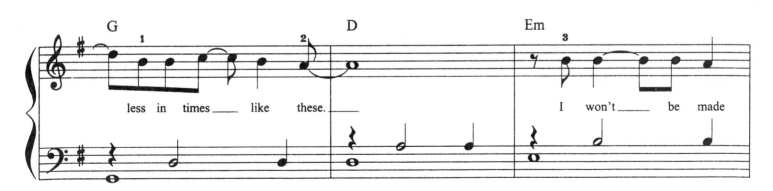

Hands - 5 - 1

104

Hands - 5 - 2

106

D.S. %· al Coda

1.2.

3.

I will get down on my knees and I will pray.

I am nev - er bro - ken. We are nev - er bro - ken. We are We are

Coda

Hands - 5 - 4

Verse 2:
Poverty stole your golden shoes,
It didn't steal your laughter.
And heartache came to visit me,
But I knew it wasn't ever after.
We'll fight not out of spite,
For someone must stand up for what's right.
'Cause where there's a man who has no voice,
There ours shall go on singing.
(To Chorus:)

Hands - 5 - 5

HAVE I TOLD YOU LATELY

Words and Music by
VAN MORRISON
Arranged by DAN COATES

ease my trou-bles, that's what you do.

There's a love that's di - vine

and it's yours and it's mine_____

like the sun.

And at the end of the day

we should give thanks and pray____

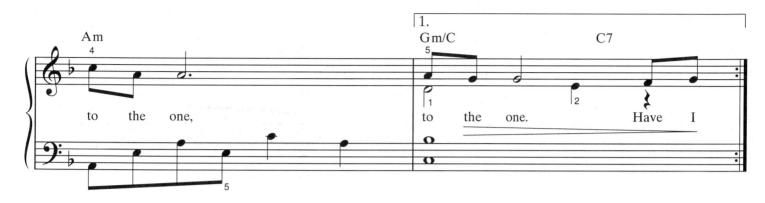

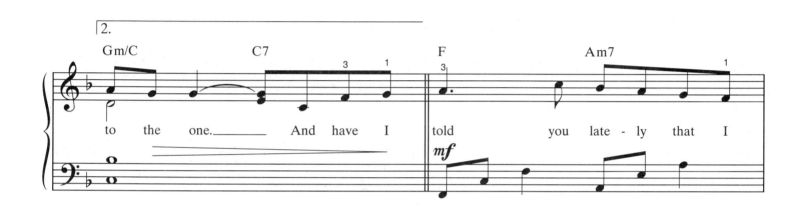

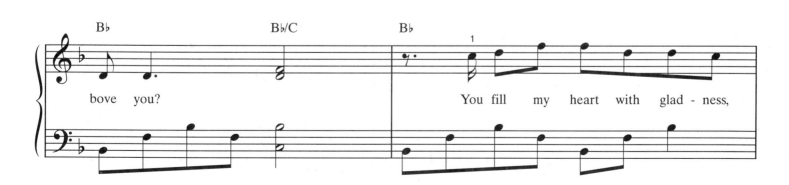

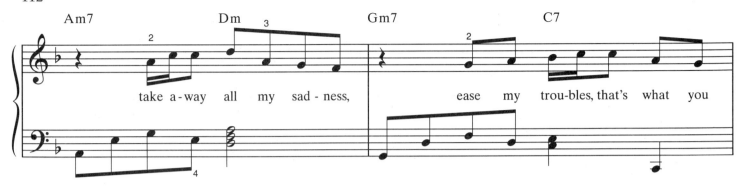

take a-way all my sad - ness, ease my trou-bles, that's what you

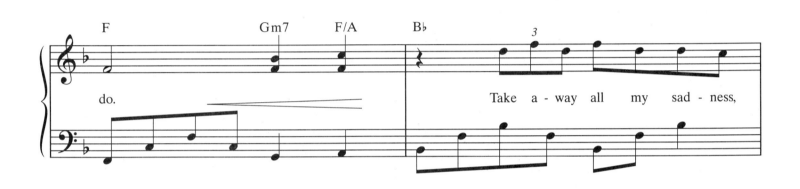

do. Take a - way all my sad - ness,

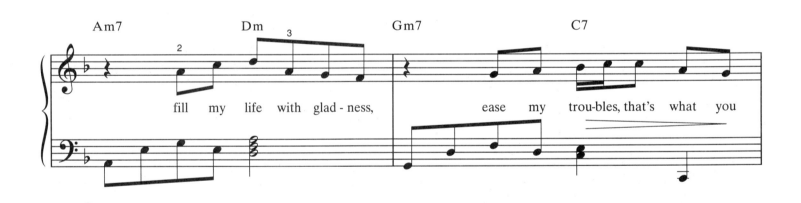

fill my life with glad - ness, ease my trou-bles, that's what you

do. *rit. e dim.*

I TURN TO YOU

Words and Music by
DIANE WARREN
Arranged by DAN COATES

Slowly (♩=76)

I Turn to You - 5 - 1

114

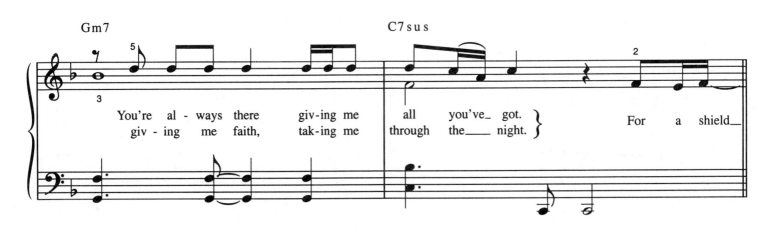

I Turn to You - 5 - 2

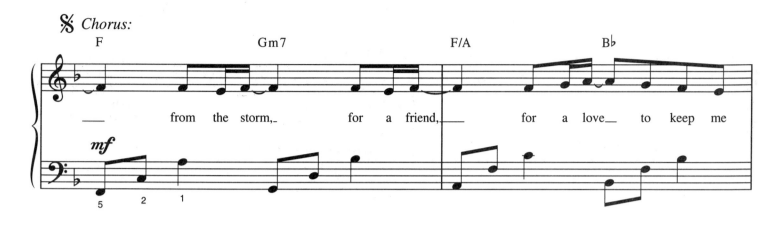

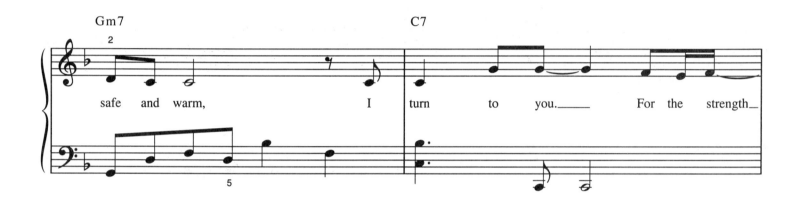

To Coda ⊕

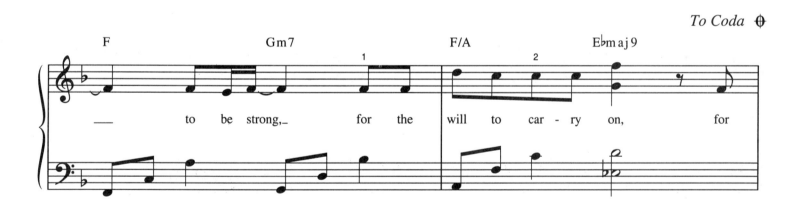

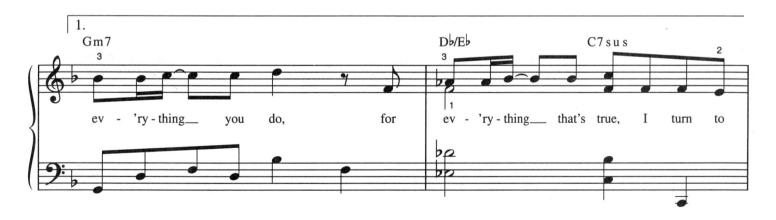

I Turn to You - 5 - 3

F   Db/Eb   C7sus

you._____   2. When I lose_

mp

2.
Gm7   C7sus   F

ev - 'ry - thing_ you do, I turn to you.

Bridge:
Ebmaj7   Dm7

For the arms to be my shel - ter through all the rain,_____   for

mf

C7sus   Eb/F   F7   Eb/F   F

truth that will nev - er change,_____   for some - one to lean

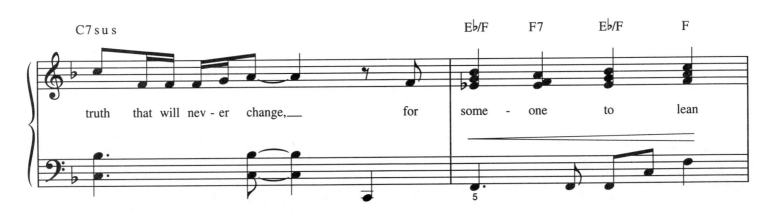

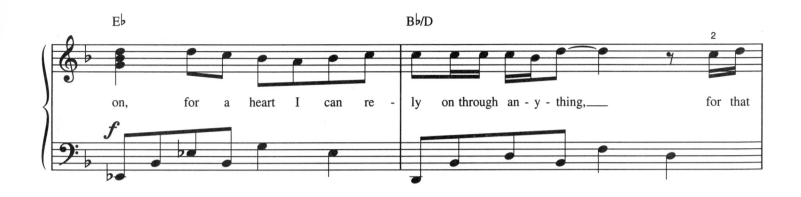

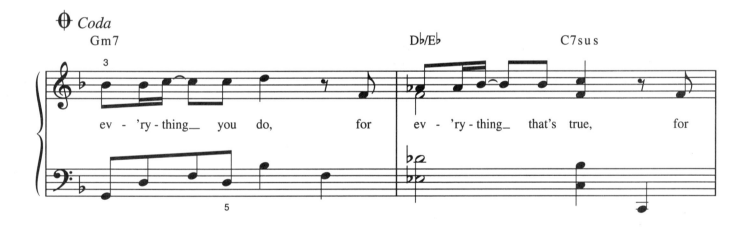

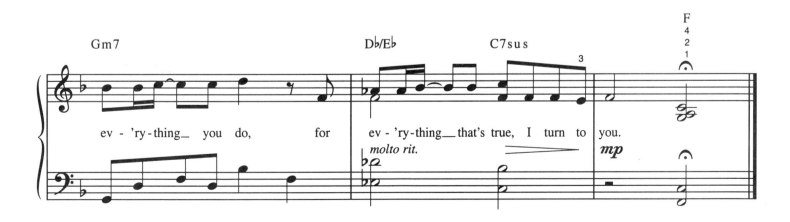

From the Original Motion Picture Soundtrack "DON JUAN DeMARCO"

HAVE YOU EVER REALLY LOVED A WOMAN?

Lyrics by
BRYAN ADAMS and ROBERT JOHN "MUTT" LANGE

Music by
MICHAEL KAMEN
Arranged by DAN COATES

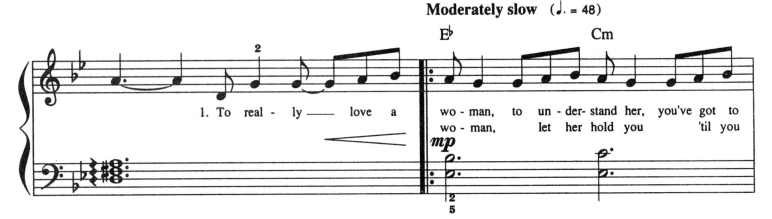

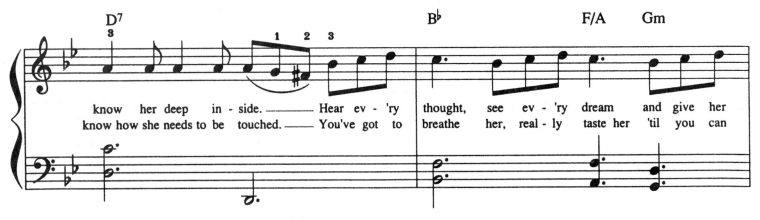

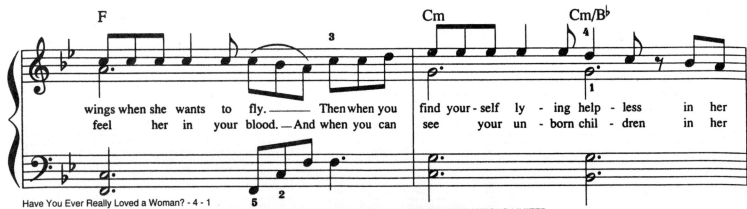

Have You Ever Really Loved a Woman? - 4 - 1

119

Have You Ever Really Loved a Woman? - 4 - 2

120

I BELIEVE I CAN FLY

Words and Music by
R. KELLY
Arranged by DAN COATES

I Believe I Can Fly - 4 - 1

124

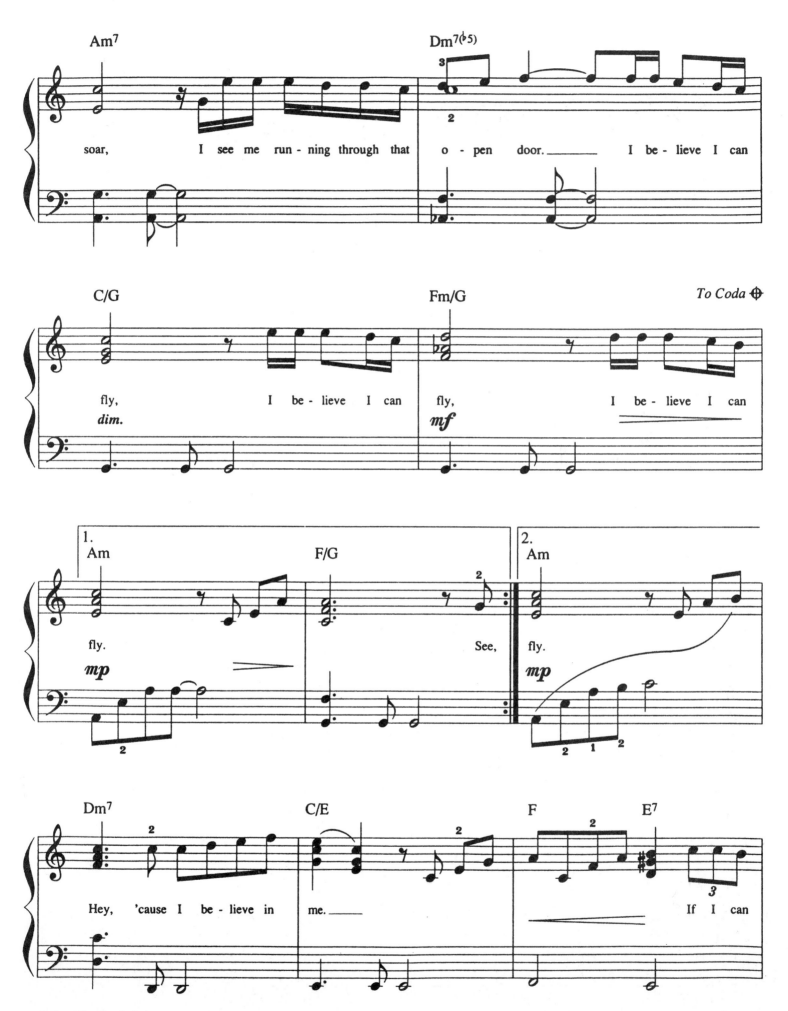

see it, _____ then I can do _____ it, if I just be-

lieve it, _____ there's noth - ing to _ it. _____ I be - lieve I can

fly. If I just spread my wings, _____ I can fly. If I just

spread my wings, _____ I can fly.

I Believe I Can Fly - 4 - 4

From the Motion Picture "THE PREACHER'S WIFE"

I BELIEVE IN YOU AND ME

Words and Music by
SANDY LINZER and DAVID WOLFERT
Arranged by DAN COATES

I Believe in You and Me - 4 - 1

128

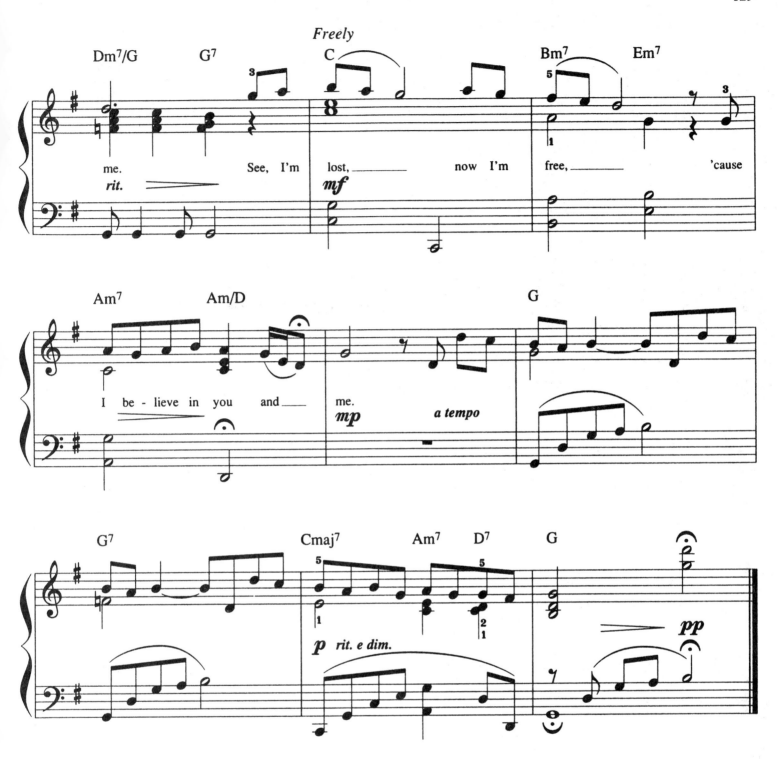

Freely

me. See, I'm lost,_____ now I'm free,_____ 'cause

rit.   *mf*

I be-lieve in you and___ me.

mp   *a tempo*

p rit. e dim.   *pp*

Verse 2:
I will never leave your side,
I will never hurt your pride.
When all the chips are down,
I will always be around
Just to be right where you are, my love.
Oh, I love you, boy.
I will never leave you out,
I will always let you in
To places no one has ever been.
Deep inside, can't you see?
I believe in you and me.

I CAN LOVE YOU LIKE THAT

Words and Music by
STEVE DIAMOND, MARIBETH DERRY
and JENNIFER KIMBALL
Arranged by DAN COATES

I Can Love You Like That - 4 - 1

I Can Love You Like That - 4 - 2

132

133

I Can Love You Like That - 4 - 4

I DO (CHERISH YOU)

Words and Music by
KEITH STEGALL and DAN HILL
Arranged by DAN COATES

Moderately slow

(with pedal)

(L.H. simile)

1. All I am, all I'll be, ev-'ry-thing in this world, all that I'll ev-er need is in your eyes, shin-ing at me. When you smile

136

Verse 2:
In my world before you,
I lived outside my emotions.
Didn't know where I was going
Till that day I found you.
How you opened my life
To a new paradise.

In a world torn by change,
Still, with all of my heart
Till my dying day,
I do cherish you.   *(To Chorus:)*

From Touchstone Pictures' "ARMAGEDDON"

I DON'T WANT TO MISS A THING

Words and Music by
DIANE WARREN
Arranged by DAN COATES

I Don't Want to Miss a Thing - 4 - 3

From the Motion Picture ''THE MIRROR HAS TWO FACES''

I FINALLY FOUND SOMEONE

Words and Music by
BARBRA STREISAND, MARVIN HAMLISCH,
R. J. LANGE and BRYAN ADAMS
Arranged by DAN COATES

I Finally Found Someone - 6 - 1

144

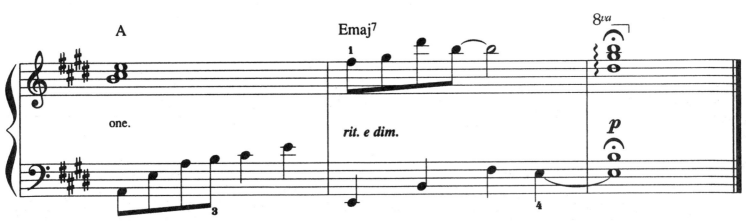

I WANT YOU TO NEED ME

Words and Music by
DIANE WARREN
Arranged by DAN COATES

Slowly, in 2 ♩ = 78

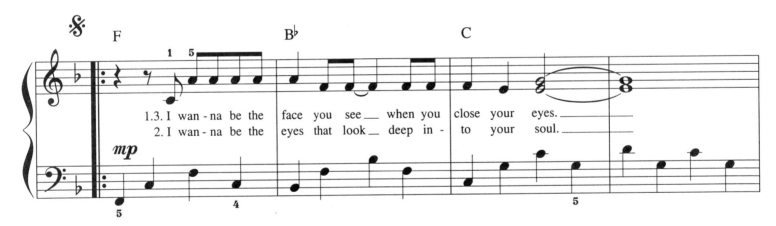

1.3. I wan-na be the face you see __ when you close your eyes. __
2. I wan-na be the eyes that look __ deep in-to your soul. __

I wan-na be the touch you need __ ev-'ry sin-gle night. __
I wan-na be the world to you. __ I just want it all. __

I Want You to Need Me - 5 - 1

150

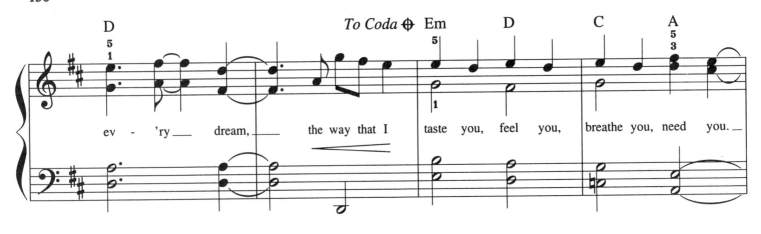

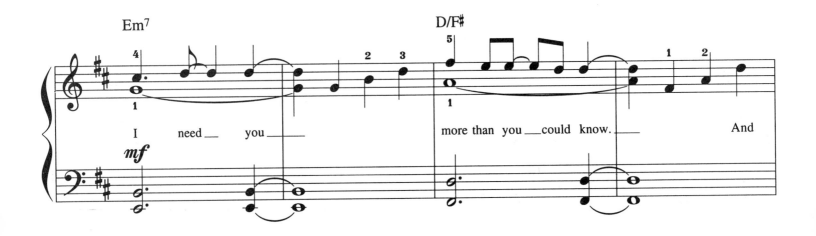

I Want You to Need Me - 5 - 3

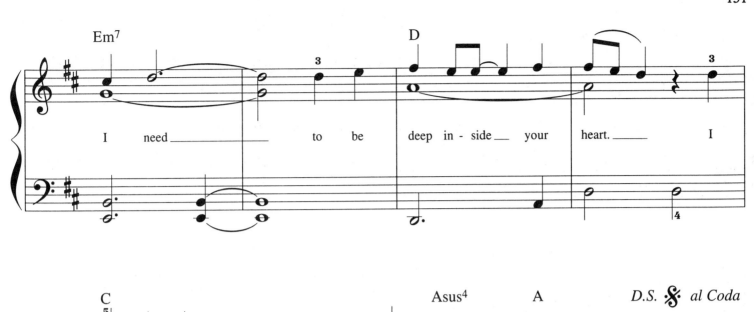

I Want You to Need Me - 5 - 4

From The Fox Searchlight Film, "THE BROTHERS McMULLEN"

I WILL REMEMBER YOU

Words and Music by
SARAH McLACHLAN, SEAMUS EGAN
and DAVID MERENDA
Arranged by DAN COATES

154

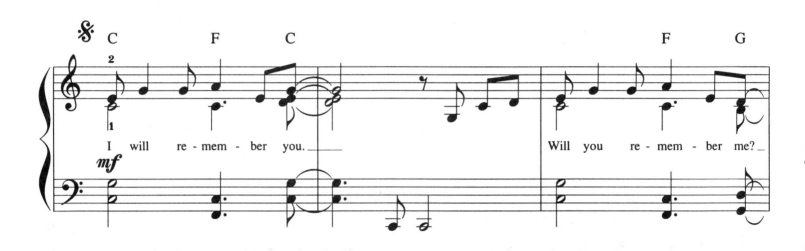

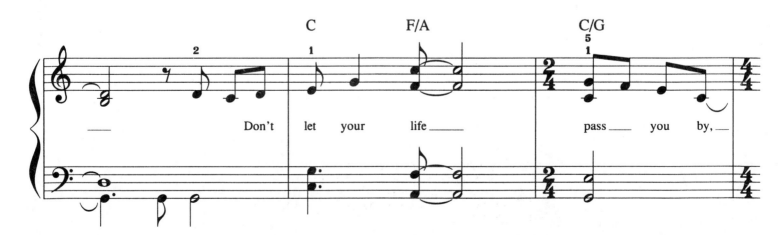

I Will Remember You - 3 - 2

Verse 2:
So afraid to love you, more afraid to lose.
I'm clinging to a past that doesn't let me choose.
Where once there was a darkness, a deep and endless night,
You gave me everything you had, oh, you gave me life.
(To Chorus:)

I WILL LOVE AGAIN

Words and Music by
PAUL BARRY and MARK TAYLOR
Arranged by DAN COATES

Moderately fast ($\quarternote = 128$)

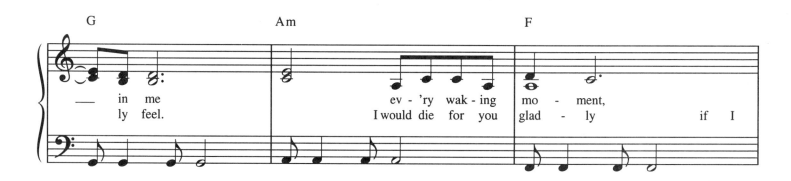

I Will Love Again - 4 - 1

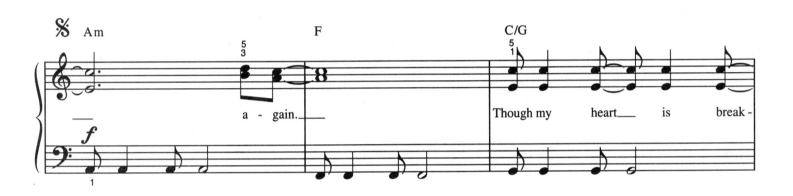

I Will Love Again - 4 - 2

To Coda ⊕

I'LL NEVER BREAK YOUR HEART

By
ALBERT MANNO and
EUGENE WILDE
Arranged by DAN COATES

I'll Never Break Your Heart - 4 - 1

162

I'll Never Break Your Heart - 4 - 3

Verse 2:
As I walked by you,
Will you get to know me
A little more better?
Girl, that's the way love goes.
And I know you're afraid
To let your feelings show,
And I understand.
But girl, it's time to let go.
I deserve a try, honey,
Just once,
Give me a chance
And I'll prove this all wrong.
You walked in,
You were so quick to judge.
But, honey, he's nothing like me.
(To Chorus:)

I'M YOUR ANGEL

Words and Music by
R. KELLY
Arranged by DAN COATES

166

I'm Your Angel - 5 - 3

168

I'm Your Angel - 5 - 5

IN THIS LIFE

Words and Music by
MIKE REID and
ALLEN SHAMBLIN
Arranged by DAN COATES

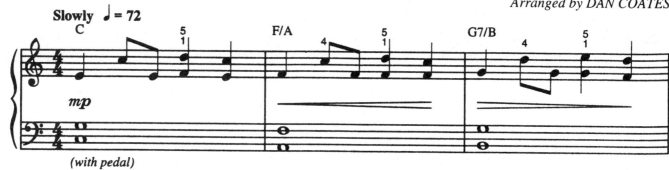

For all I'd been blessed with in my life,

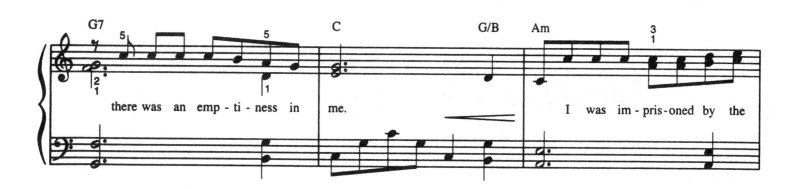

there was an emp-ti-ness in me. I was im-pris-oned by the

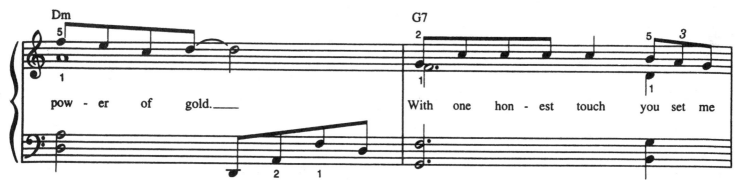

pow-er of gold.___ With one hon-est touch you set me

In This Life - 3 - 1

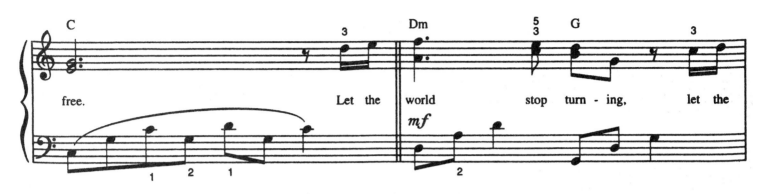

free.   Let the   world   stop turn - ing,   let the

sun   stop burn - ing.   Let them   tell   me   love's   not   worth___   go - ing

through.   If   it   all   falls   a - part,   I will

know deep   in   my   heart   the   on - ly   dream   that   mat - tered   had   come

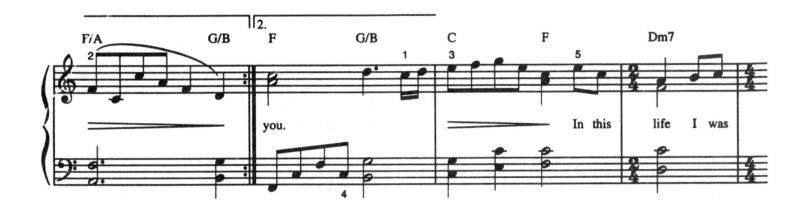

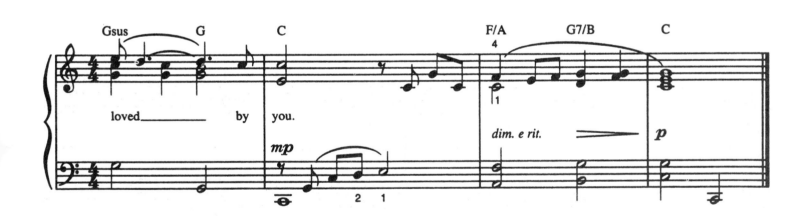

Verse 2:
For every mountain I have climbed,
Every raging river crossed,
You were the treasure that I longed to find.
Without your love I would be lost.
(To Chorus:)

KISS THE RAIN

Words and Music by
ERIC BAZILIAN, DESMOND CHILD
and BILLIE MYERS
Arranged by DAN COATES

Kiss the Rain - 4 - 1

try - ing to ____ ex - plain. Some - thing's wrong, ____ you just don't sound ____

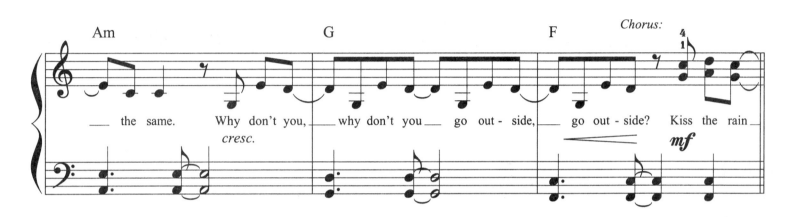

____ the same. Why don't you, why don't you ____ go out - side, ____ go out - side? Kiss the rain ____

____ when - ev - er you need ____ me. Kiss the rain ____ when - ev - er I'm gone ____

____ too long. If your lips ____ feel lone - ly and thirst - y, ____ kiss the rain ____

174

Kiss the Rain - 4 - 3

Verse 2:
Hello? Do you miss me?
I hear you say you do,
But not the way I'm missing you.
What's new? How's the weather?
Is it stormy where you are?
You sound so close,
But it feels like you're so far.
Oh, would it mean anything
If you knew what I'm left imagining
In my mind, in my mind.
Would you go, would you go...
(To Chorus:)

Kiss the Rain - 4 - 4

LARGER THAN LIFE

Words and Music by
MAX MARTIN, KRISTIAN LUNDIN
and BRIAN T. LITTRELL
Arranged by DAN COATES

Larger Than Life - 4 - 1

Larger Than Life - 4 - 2

178

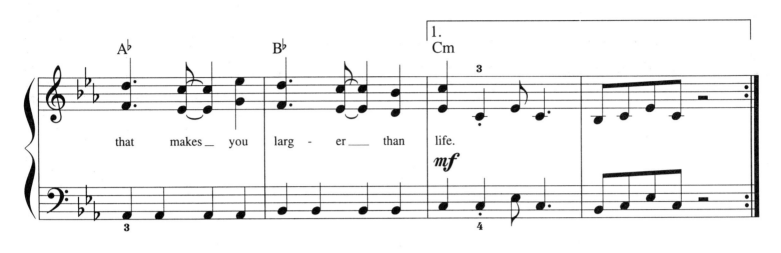

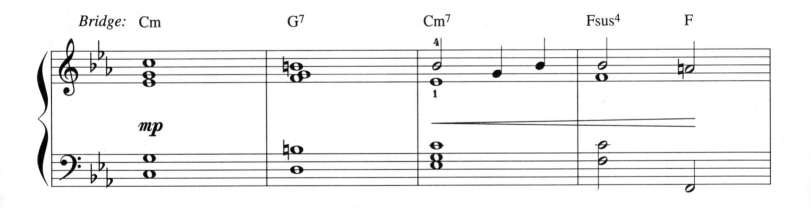

Larger Than Life - 4 - 3

(GOD MUST HAVE SPENT)
A LITTLE MORE TIME ON YOU

Words and Music by
CARL STURKEN and EVAN ROGERS
Arranged by DAN COATES

(God Must Have Spent) a Little More Time on You - 4 - 1

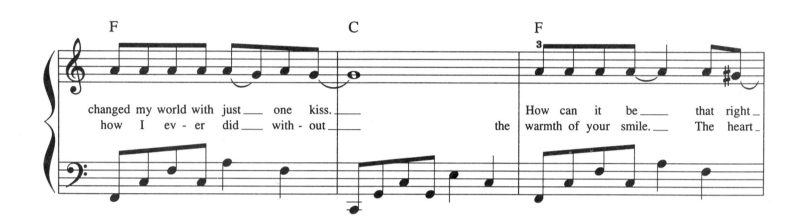

(God Must Have Spent) a Little More Time on You - 4 - 2

(God Must Have Spent) a Little More Time on You - 4 - 4

A LOVE UNTIL
THE END OF TIME

Lyric by
CAROL CONNORS

Music by
LEE HOLDRIDGE
Arranged by DAN COATES

A Love Until the End of Time - 3 - 1

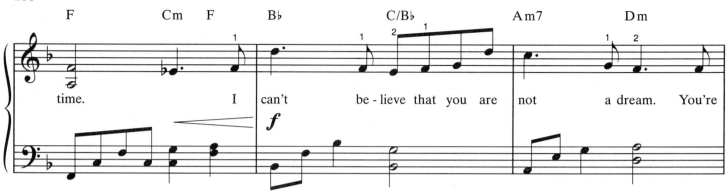

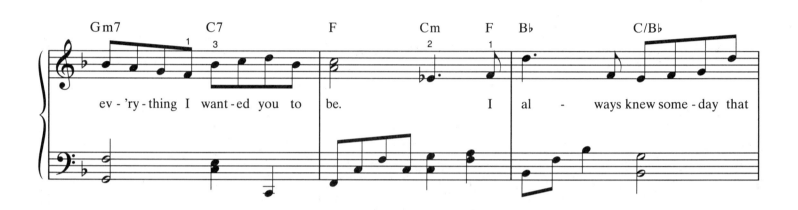

MENTAL PICTURE

Words and Music by
JON SECADA and
MIGUEL A. MOREJON
Arranged by DAN COATES

Verse 2:
Time was of the essence,
And as usual the day turns into minutes.
Sharing love and tenderness,
That's the nerve you struck in me that sent a signal.
To the other side,
(Girl, I don't know)
Saying my blind side.
And if a ...   (To Chorus:)

LOVE WILL KEEP US ALIVE

Words and Music by
JIM CAPALDI, PETER VALE
and PAUL CARRACK
Arranged by DAN COATES

Love Will Keep Us Alive - 4 - 1

192

From the Miramax Motion Picture "Music Of The Heart"

MUSIC OF MY HEART

Words and Music by
DIANE WARREN
Arranged by DAN COATES

Slowly, with feeling

1. You'll nev - er know _____ what you've
2. You were the one _____ al - ways

done for me, _____ what your faith in me has
on my side, _____ al - ways stand - ing by,

done for my soul. _____ You'll nev - er know ____ the gift you've
see - ing me through. _____ You were the song ____ that al - ways

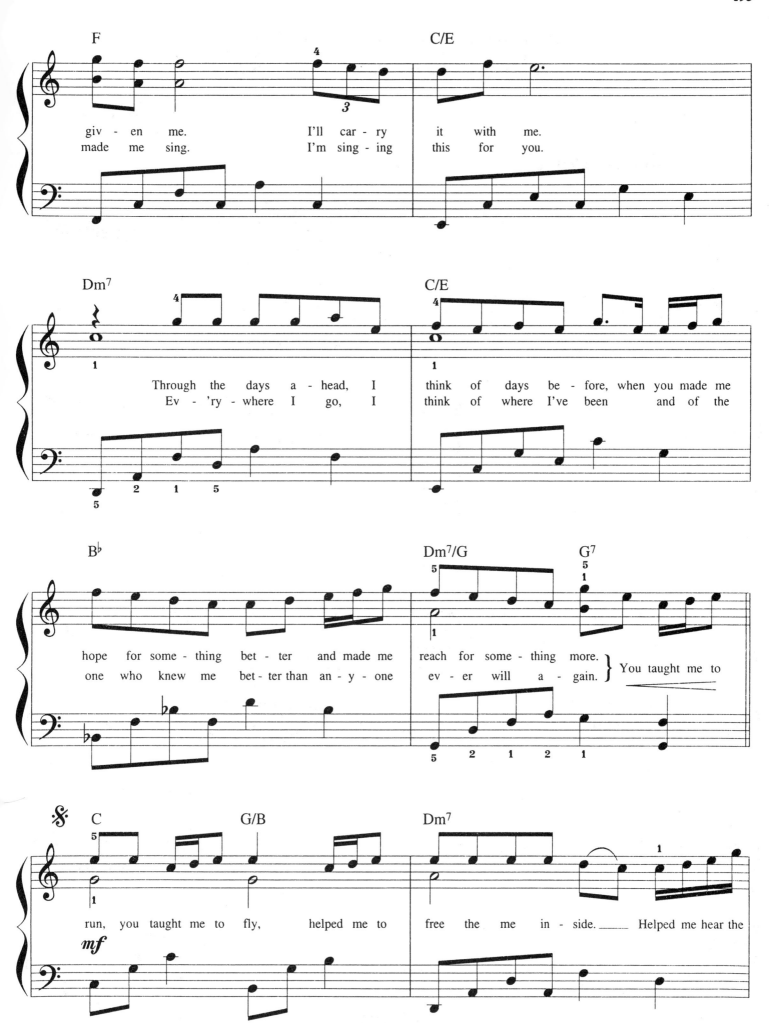

MY ONE TRUE FRIEND

(From "ONE TRUE THING")

Words and Music by
CAROLE BAYER SAGER, CAROLE KING
and DAVID FOSTER
Arranged by DAN COATES

were the light in-side of me.

dim.

meno mosso

f a tempo

I have

walked _____ and I have prayed _____ I could for-

NOW AND FOREVER

Music and Lyrics by
RICHARD MARX
Arranged by DAN COATES

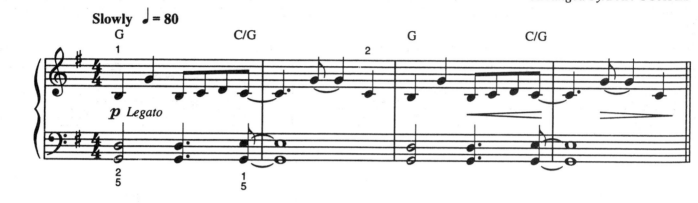

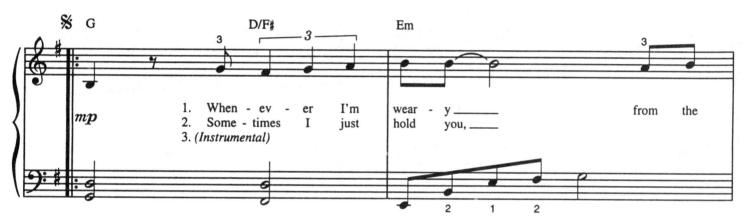

1. When - ev - er I'm wear - y _____ from the
2. Some - times I just hold you, _____
3. *(Instrumental)*

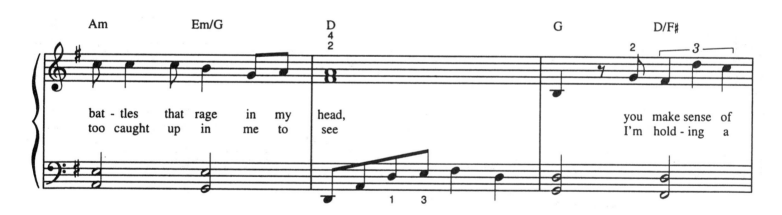

bat - tles that rage in my head, you make sense of
too caught up in me to see I'm hold - ing a

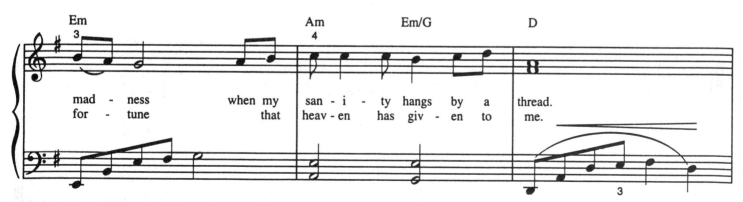

mad - ness when my san - i - ty hangs by a thread.
for - tune that heav - en has giv - en to me.

Now and Forever - 3 - 1

204

Now and Forever - 3 - 2

OH HOW THE YEARS GO BY

Words and Music by
WILL JENNINGS anf SIMON CLIMIE
Arranged by DAN COATES

Oh How the Years Go By - 4 - 1

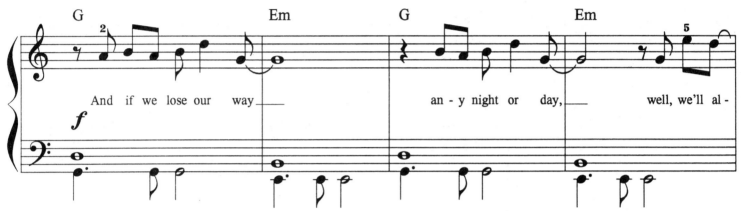

209

Verse 2:
There were times we stumbled,
They thought they had us down,
We came around.
How we rolled and rambled,
We got lost and we got found.
Now we're back on solid ground.
We took everything
All our times would bring
In this world of danger.
'Cause when your heart is strong,
You know you're not alone
In this world of strangers.
(To Chorus:)

Oh How the Years Go By - 4 - 4

ON MY OWN

Words and Music by
CAROLE BAYER SAGER and BURT BACHARACH
Arranged by DAN COATES

Moderately Slow

On My Own - 5 - 1

said our love would al - ways be true.___
now I know what lov - ing you cost.___

Some-thing in my heart al - ways knew I'd be
Now we're up to talk - in' di - vorce and we

To Coda ⊕

ly - ing here be - side you.___
were - n't e - ven mar - ried.___

On my
On my

own,___ on my own,___
own,___ once a - gain,___

mf

212

214

Coda

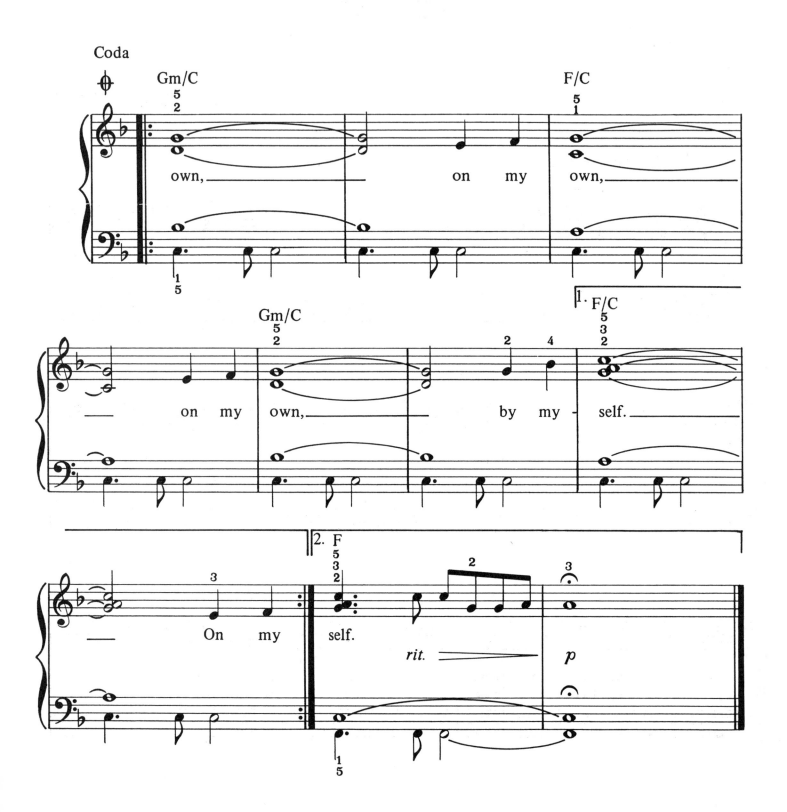

Extra Lyrics:

3. So many times
   I know I could have told you;
   Losin' you, it cuts like a knife.
   You walked out and there went my life;
   I don't want to live without you.
   On my own, *etc.*

THE ONE

Words and Music by
MAX MARTIN and BRIAN T. LITTRELL
Arranged by DAN COATES

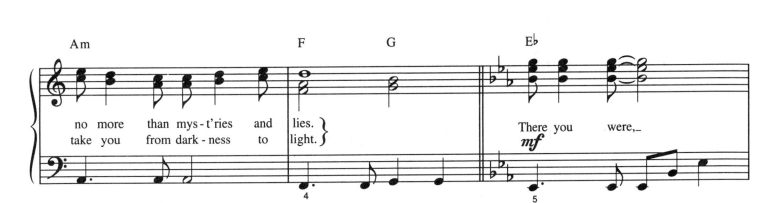

The One - 5 - 1

216

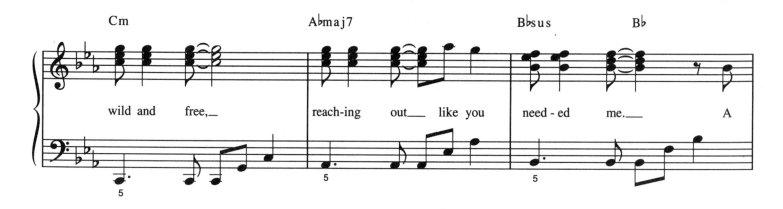

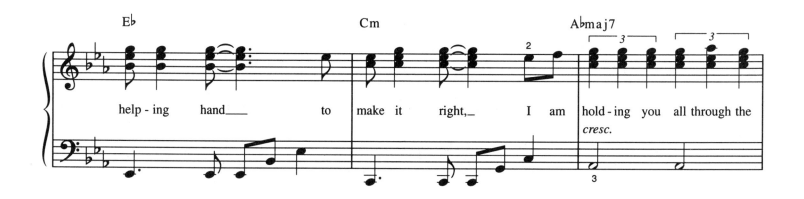

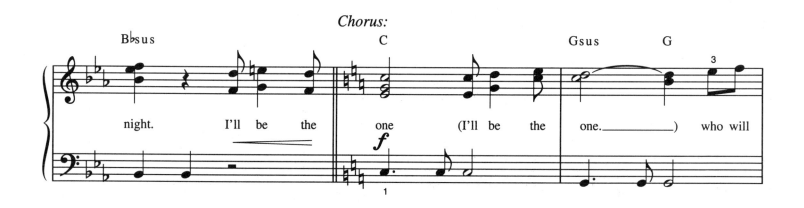

The One - 5 - 2

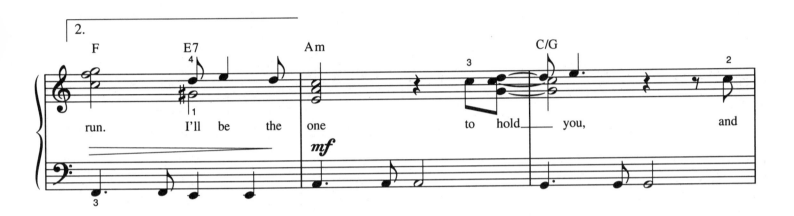

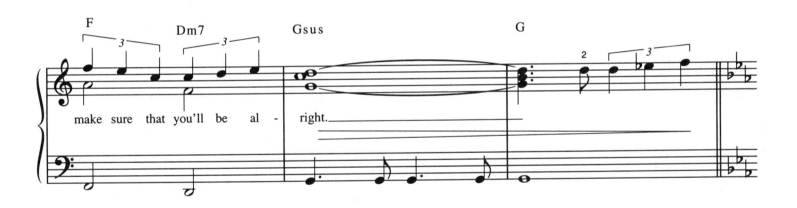

Bridge:

The One - 5 - 3

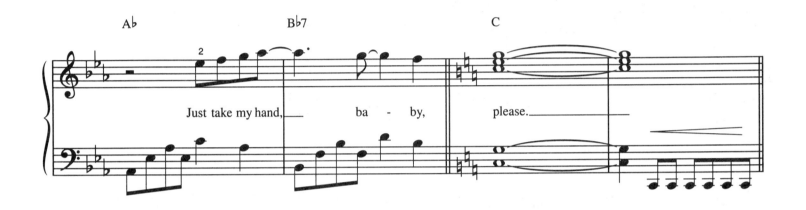

Chorus:

The One - 5 - 5

From the TriStar Pictures Feature Film "ONLY YOU"

ONCE IN A LIFETIME

Words and Music by
WALTER AFANASIEFF, MICHAEL BOLTON
and DIANE WARREN
Arranged by DAN COATES

Once in a Lifetime - 4 - 1

222

To Coda

Once in a Lifetime - 4 - 3

THE PRAYER

Words and Music by
CAROLE BAYER SAGER and DAVID FOSTER
Arranged by DAN COATES

Slowly, with expression ♩ = 72

QUIT PLAYING GAMES
(With My Heart)

Words and Music by
MAX MARTIN and HERBERT CRICHLOW
Arranged by DAN COATES

Bright rock tempo

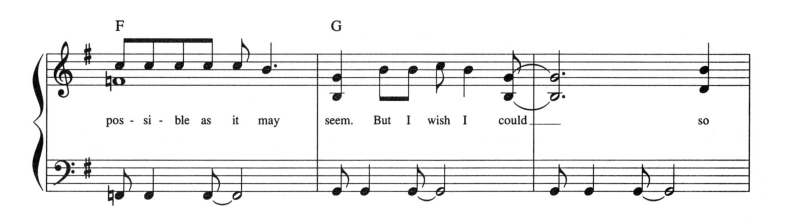

Quit Playing Games - 4 - 2

228

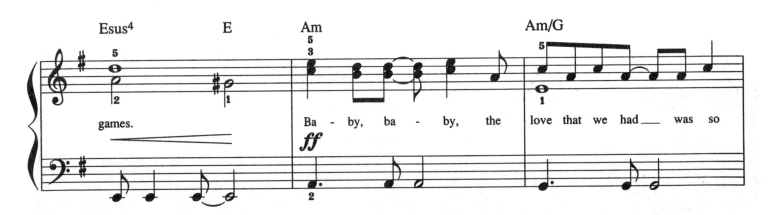

SAVE THE BEST FOR LAST

Words and Music by
WENDY WALDMAN, JON LIND
and PHIL GALDSTON
Arranged by DAN COATES

Save the Best for Last - 4 - 1

232

Additional Lyrics

Sometimes the snow comes down in June,
Sometimes the sun goes 'round the moon.
Just when I thought our chance had passed,
You go and save the best for last.

Save the Best for Last - 4 - 4

SHOW ME THE MEANING
OF BEING LONELY

Words and Music by
MAX MARTIN and HERBERT CRICHLOW
Arranged by DAN COATES

Moderately slow

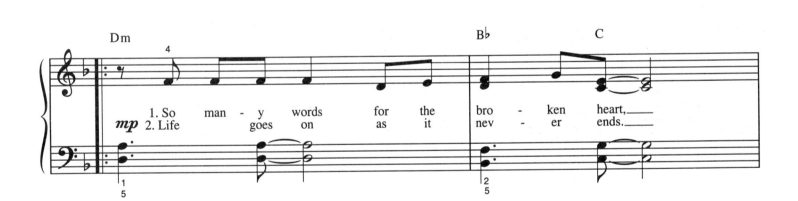

1. So man-y words for the bro-ken heart,
2. Life goes on as it nev-er ends.

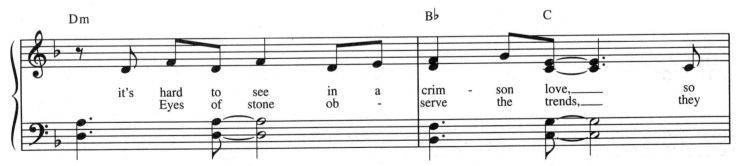

it's hard to see in a crim-son love, so
Eyes of stone ob- serve the trends, they

Show Me the Meaning of Being Lonely - 5 - 1

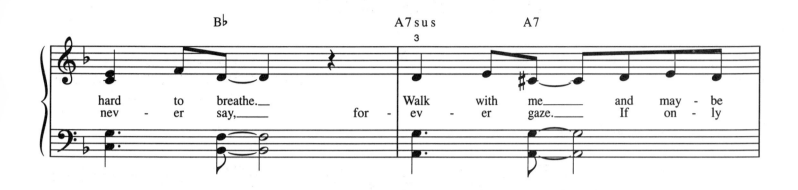

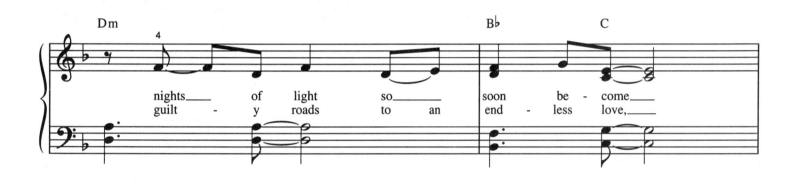

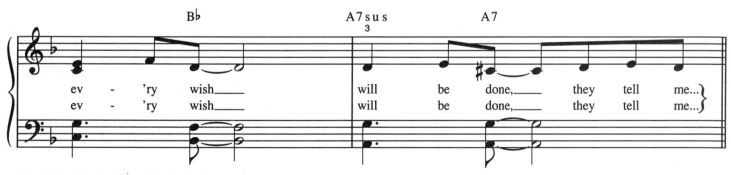

Show Me the Meaning of Being Lonely - 5 - 2

236

Show Me the Meaning of Being Lonely - 5 - 3

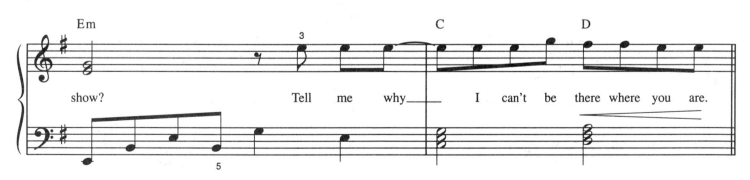

Show Me the Meaning of Being Lonely - 5 - 4

SOMETHING ABOUT THE WAY
YOU LOOK TONIGHT

Lyrics by
BERNIE TAUPIN

Music by
ELTON JOHN
Arranged by DAN COATES

Something About the Way You Look Tonight - 3 - 1

Am7
Dm
F/C
light up ev - 'ry sec - ond of the day, but in the
pull the deep - est sec - rets from my heart. In all
B♭
Gm7
C
moon - light you just shine like a bea - con on the bay.
hon - es - ty, I'm speech - less and don't know where to start.
cresc.
F
A7
And I can't ex - plain but it's some - thing a - bout the way you
f
Dm
D7
Gm
look to - night. It takes my breath a - way. It's that
Gm7
C
feel - ing I get a - bout you deep in - side. And I can't de -

Something About the Way You Look Tonight - 3 - 3

SMOOTH

Music and Lyrics by
ITAAL SHUR and ROB THOMAS
Arranged by DAN COATES

Smooth - 4 - 1

'Cause you're so smooth. Oh, and it's

Chorus:

just like the o - cean un - der the moon.__ Well, it's the same as the e - mo - tion that I

get from you._____ You got the kind of lov - ing that can be so smooth,__ yeah.

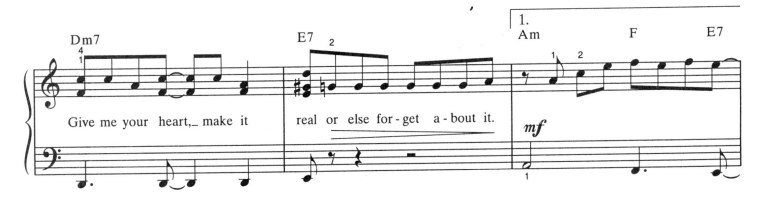

Give me your heart,__ make it real or else for - get a - bout it.

1.
Am   F   E7

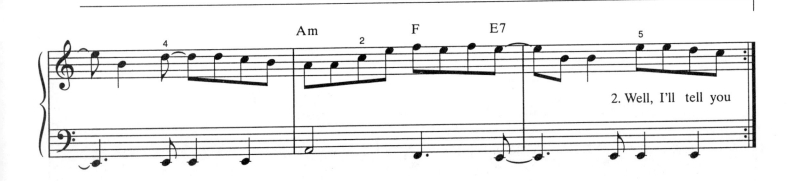

2. Well, I'll tell you

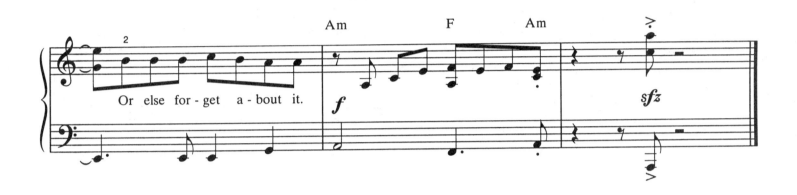

Verse 2:
Well, I'll tell you one thing,
If you should leave, it'd be a crying shame.
In every breath and every word
I hear your name calling me out, yeah.
Well, out from the barrio,
You hear my rhythm on your radio.
You feel the tugging of the world,
So soft and slow, turning you 'round and 'round.
And if you said this life ain't good enough,
I would give my world to lift you up.
I could change my life to better suit your mood.
'Cause you're so smooth.
(To Chorus:)

From the Tri-Star Motion Picture ''PHILADELPHIA''

STREETS OF PHILADELPHIA

Words and Music by
BRUCE SPRINGSTEEN
Arranged by DAN COATES

Streets of Philadelphia - 3 - 1

Verse 2:
I walked the avenue 'til my legs felt like stone.
I heard the voices of friends vanished and gone.
At night I could hear the blood in my veins
Just as black and whispering as the rain
On the streets of Philadelphia.

Verse 3:
The night has fallen, I'm lyin' awake.
I can feel myself fading away.
So, receive me, brother, with your faithless kiss,
Or will we leave each other alone like this
On the streets of Philadelphia?

THE SWEETEST DAYS

Words and Music by
WENDY WALDMAN, JON LIND
and PHIL GALDSTON
Arranged by DAN COATES

The Sweetest Days - 3 - 1

250

The Sweetest Days - 3 - 2

The Sweetest Days - 3 - 3

TAKE A BOW

Words and Music by
MADONNA CICCONE and BABYFACE
Arranged by DAN COATES

Take a Bow - 4 - 1

254

Take a Bow - 4 - 3

TEARS IN HEAVEN

Words and Music by
ERIC CLAPTON and WILL JENNINGS
Arranged by DAN COATES

Tears in Heaven - 4 - 1

Tears in Heaven - 4 - 2

258

TELL HIM

Words and Music by
LINDA THOMPSON, DAVID FOSTER
and WALTER AFANASIEFF
Arranged by DAN COATES

Slowly ♩ = 76

1. I'm scared, so a-fraid to show I care. Will he think me weak if I trem-ble when I speak? What if there's an-oth-er one he's think-ing of?

Tell Him - 5 - 1

264

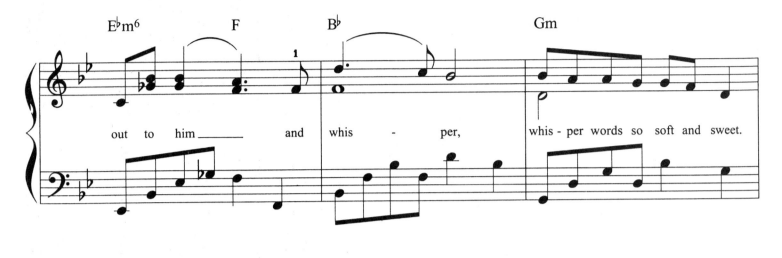

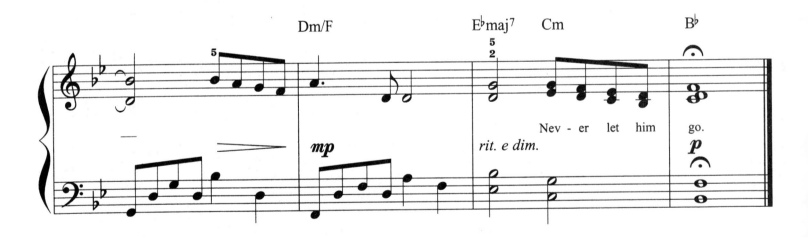

Verse 2:
(Barbra:)
Touch him with the gentleness you feel inside.
Your love can't be denied.
The truth will set you free.
You'll have what's meant to be.
All in time, you'll see.
(Celine:)
I love him,
Of that much I can be sure.
I don't think I could endure
If I let him walk away
When I have so much to say.
(To Chorus:)

TO LOVE YOU MORE

Words and Music by
JUNIOR MILES and DAVID FOSTER
Arranged by DAN COATES

Slowly, with expression

To Love You More - 5 - 1

THAT'S THE WAY IT IS

Words and Music by
MAX MARTIN, KRISTIAN LUNDIN
and ANDREAS CARLSSON
Arranged by DAN COATES

That's the Way It Is - 4 - 1

___

That's the Way It Is - 4 - 2

That's the Way It Is - 4 - 4

TOO LATE, TOO SOON

Words and Music by
JON SECADA, JAMES HARRIS III
and TERRY LEWIS
Arranged by DAN COATES

Too Late, Too Soon - 3 - 1

Verse 2:
I wish I would have known,
I wouldn't have left you all alone.
Temptation led you wrong.
Tell me how long this has been goin' on?
'Cause I thought our love was strong,
But I guess I must be dreamin'.
(To Chorus:)

UN-BREAK MY HEART

Words and Music by
DIANE WARREN
Arranged by DAN COATES

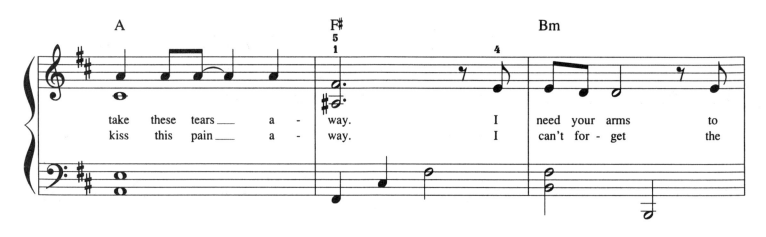

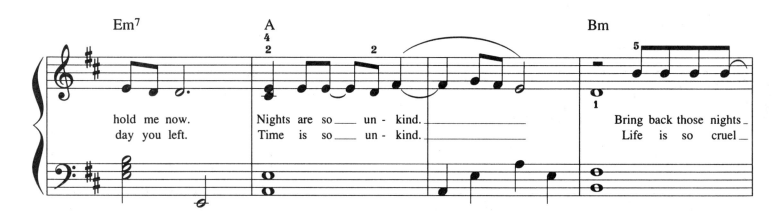

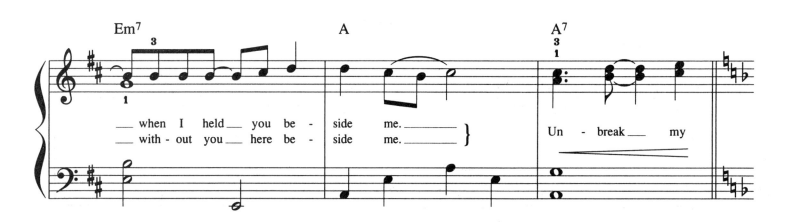

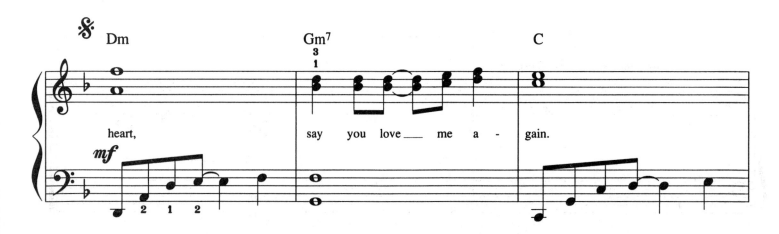

Un-Break My Heart - 5 - 2

280

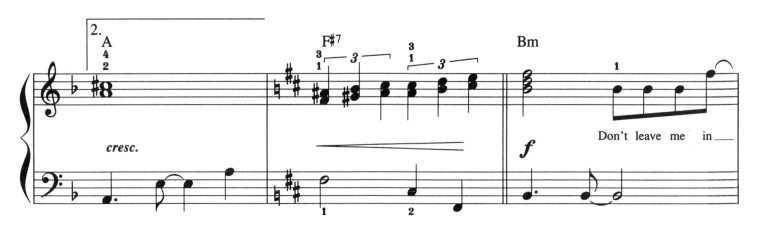

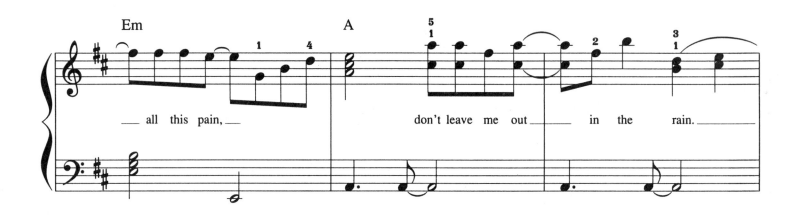

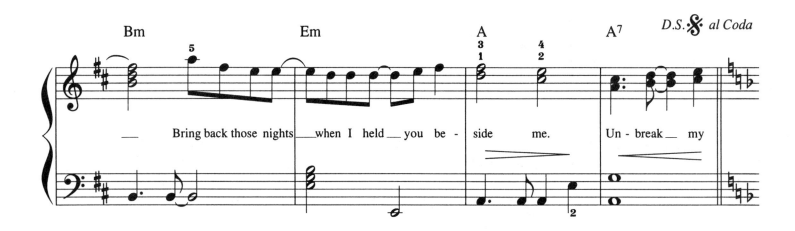

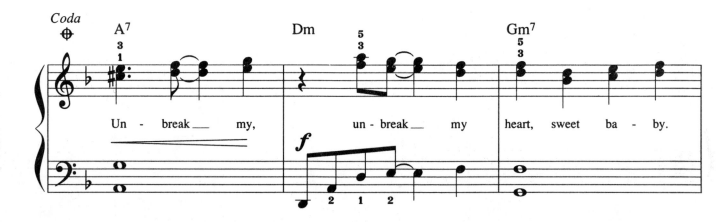

Un-Break My Heart - 5 - 4

Un-Break My Heart - 5 - 5

VALENTINE

Composed by
JIM BRICKMAN and JACK KUGELL
Arranged by DAN COATES

Verse 2:
All of my life,
I have been waiting for all you give to me.
You've opened my eyes
And shown me how to love unselfishly.
I've dreamed of this a thousand times before,
But in my dreams I couldn't love you more.
I will give you my heart until the end of time.
You're all I need, my love,
My Valentine.

WHERE DOES MY HEART BEAT NOW

Words and Music by
TAYLOR RHODES and
ROBERT WHITE JOHNSON
Arranged by DAN COATES

WHEREVER YOU GO

Words and Music by
DURELL BOTTOMS, NICOLE RENEE
and MICHAEL McCRARY
Arranged by DAN COATES

ev - 'ry - thing.___ Who will love me? Who will care?

Who will be there when I need___ some - one for me? Who will be there to dry my

eyes when I go down on my knees? I need you to say: Where - ev - er you go,___

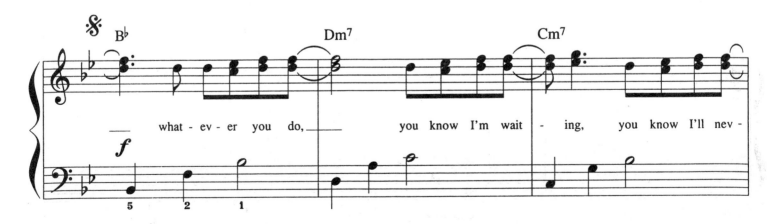

what - ev - er you do,___ you know I'm wait - ing, you know I'll nev -

Wherever You Go - 6 - 5

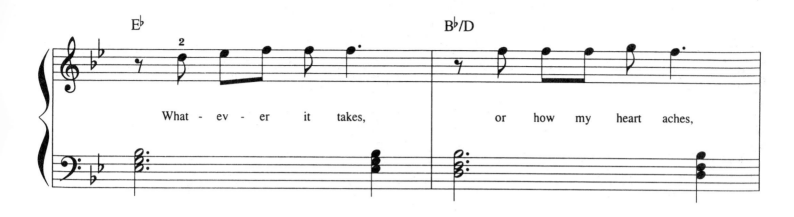

Whatever it takes, or how my heart aches,

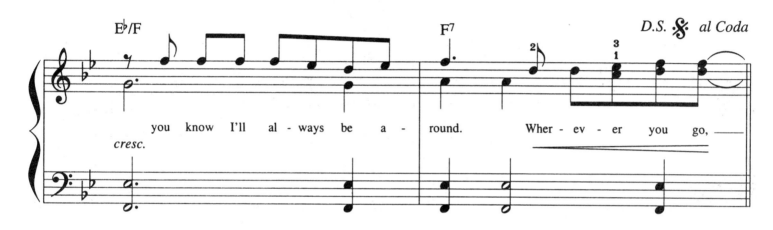

you know I'll always be around. Wherever you go,

cresc.

D.S. 𝄋 al Coda

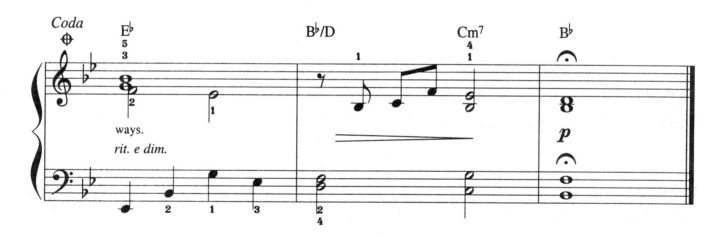

Coda

ways.

rit. e dim.

p

Verse 2:
Goodbye is such a hard thing to say
When you're all I know,
When you're my everything.
And who will stay and care for me?
When you're gone, I'll be all alone.
Who will come and comfort me
And fulfill my needs?
Who will love me?
Who will care?
Who will be there
When I need someone for me?
Who will be there to dry my eyes
When I go down on my knees?
I need you to say:
(To Chorus:)

YOU ARE NOT ALONE

Written and Composed by
R. KELLY
Arranged by DAN COATES

You Are Not Alone - 5 - 1

299

You Are Not Alone - 5 - 4

300

YOU MUST LOVE ME

Words by TIM RICE
Music by ANDREW LLOYD WEBBER
Arranged by DAN COATES

You Must Love Me - 3 -1

303

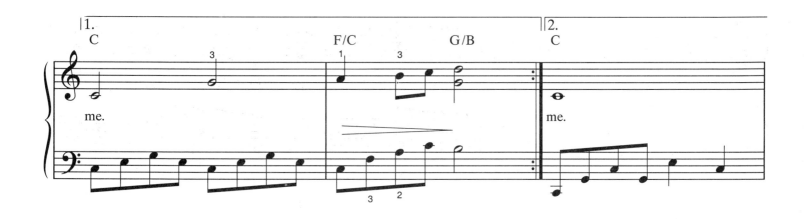

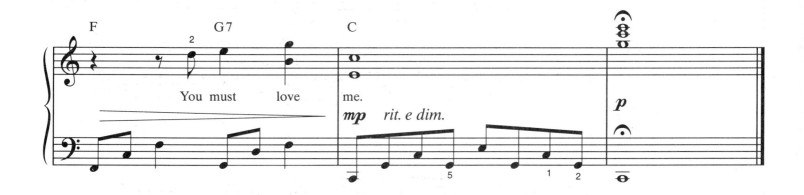

Verse 2:
(Instrumental solo for 8 measures)
Why are you at my side?
How can I be any use to you now?
Give me a chance and I'll let you see how
Nothing has changed.
Deep in my heart I'm concealing
Things that I'm longing to say,
Scared to confess what I'm feeling,
Frightened you'll slip away.
You must love me.

You Must Love Me - 3 - 3

YOU GOT IT

Words and Music by
ROY ORBISON, TOM PETTY
and JEFF LYNNE
Arranged by DAN COATES

You Got It - 4 - 1

YOU'LL SEE

Words and Music by
MADONNA CICCONE and
DAVID FOSTER
Arranged by DAN COATES

You'll See - 4 - 1

309

You'll See - 4 - 2

Verse 2:
You think that I can never laugh again,
You'll see.
You think that you've destroyed my faith in love.
You think after all you've done,
I'll never find my way back home.
You'll see, somehow, some day.   *(To Chorus:)*

Verse 3:
You think that you are strong, but you are weak,
You'll see.
It takes more strength to cry, admit defeat.
I have truth on my side,
You only have deceit.
You'll see, somehow, some day.   *(To Chorus:)*

YOU WERE MEANT FOR ME

Words and Music by
JEWEL KILCHER and STEVE POLTZ
Arranged by DAN COATES

Moderate swing feel

I hear the clock, it's six A. M., __

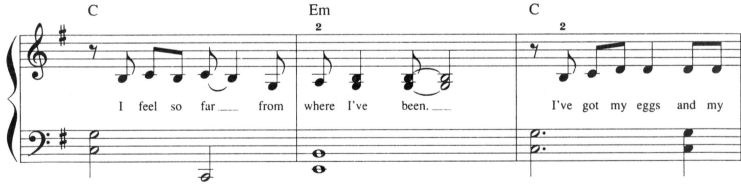

I feel so far __ from where I've been. __ I've got my eggs and my

pan- cakes, too, ___ I've got ma- ple syr- up, ev- 'ry- thing but you. __

You Were Meant for Me - 5 - 1

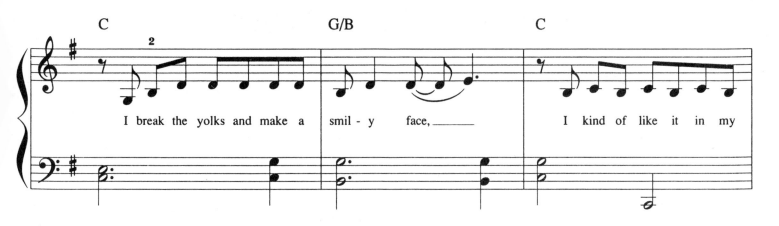

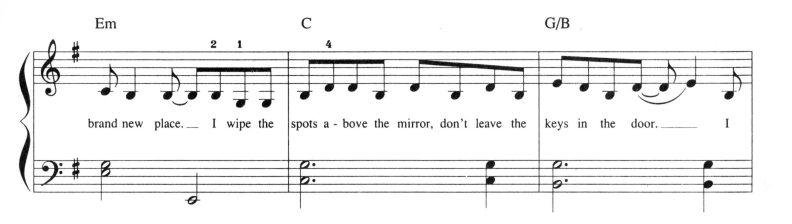

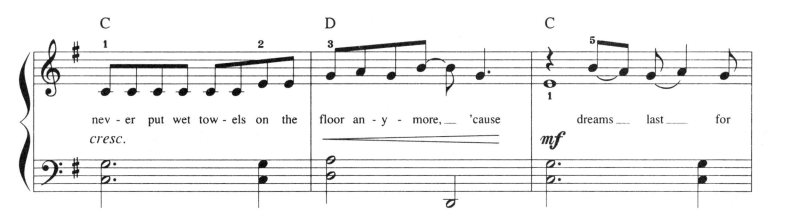

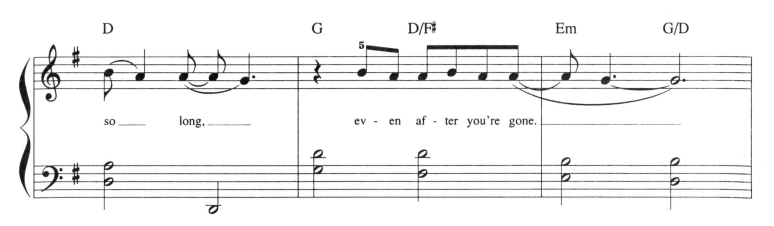

You Were Meant for Me - 5 - 2

314

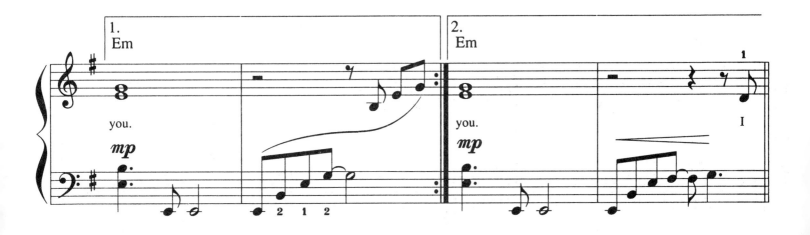

You Were Meant for Me - 5 - 3

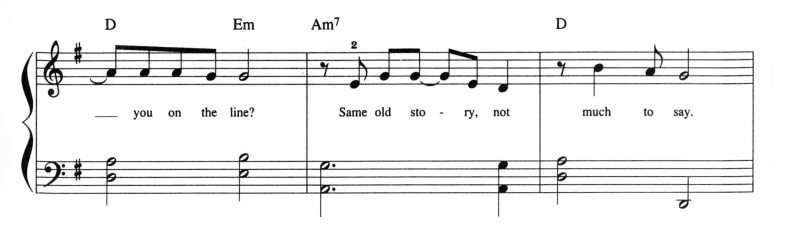

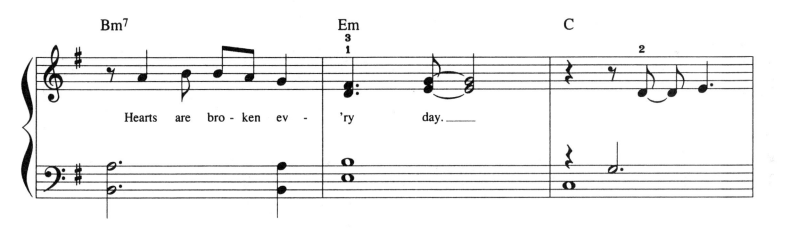

D.S. 𝄋 *al Coda*

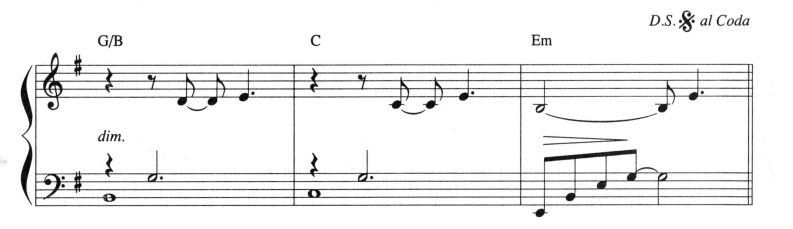

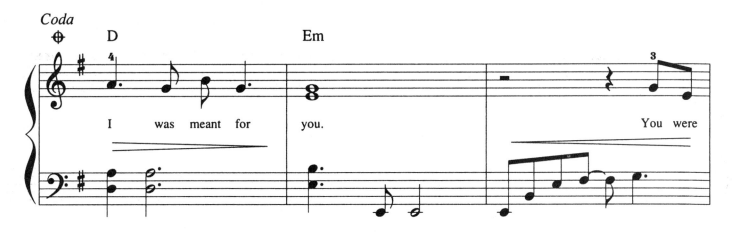

C   D   C

meant for me   and   I   was meant for   you.

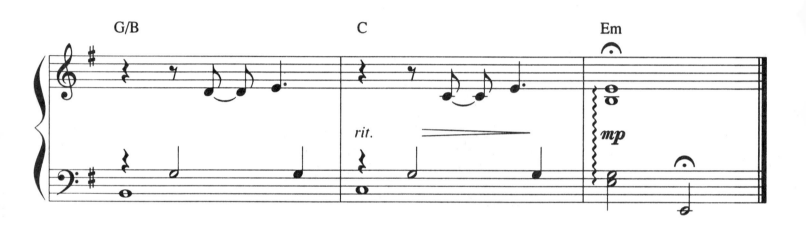

G/B   C   Em

rit.

mp

Verse 2:
I called my mama, she was out for a walk.
Consoled a cup of coffee, but it didn't wanna talk.
So I picked up a paper, it was more bad news,
More hearts being broken or people being used.
Put on my coat in the pouring rain.
I saw a movie, it just wasn't the same,
'Cause it was happy and I was sad,
And it made me miss you, oh, so bad.
(To Chorus:)

Verse 3:
I brush my teeth and put the cap back on,
I know you hate it when I leave the light on.
I pick a book up and then I turn the sheets down,
And then I take a breath and a good look around.
Put on my pj's and hop into bed.
I'm half alive but I feel mostly dead.
I try and tell myself it'll be all right,
I just shouldn't think anymore tonight.
(To Chorus:)